A2 Chemistry
UNIT 5

LRC Stoke Park
GUILDFORD COLLEGE

Edexcel

Unit 5: Transition Metals, Quantitative Kinetics and Applied Organic Chemistry

George Facer

153449

547 FAC

Philip Allan Updates
Market Place
Deddington
Oxfordshire
OX15 0SE

Orders
Bookpoint Ltd, 130 Milton Park, Abingdon, Oxfordshire, OX14 4SB
tel: 01235 827720
fax: 01235 400454
e-mail: uk.orders@bookpoint.co.uk
Lines are open 9.00 a.m.–5.00 p.m., Monday to Saturday, with a 24-hour message
answering service. You can also order through the Philip Allan Updates website:
www.philipallan.co.uk

© Philip Allan Updates 2003

ISBN-13: 978-0-86003-874-0
ISBN-10: 0-86003-874-2

This guide has been written specifically to support students preparing for
the Edexcel A2 Chemistry Unit 5 examination. The content has been neither
approved nor endorsed by Edexcel/London Qualifications and remains the
sole responsibility of the author. Exam questions are reproduced by permission
of London Qualifications. London Qualifications accepts no responsibility
whatsoever for the accuracy or method of working in the answers given.

Printed by MPG Books, Bodmin

Contents

Introduction

■ ■ ■

Content Guidance

■ ■ ■

Questions and Answers

Introduction

About this guide

This unit guide is one of a series covering the Edexcel specification for AS and A2 chemistry. It offers advice for the effective study of **Unit 5: Transition Metals, Quantitative Kinetics and Applied Organic Chemistry**. Its aim is to help you *understand* the chemistry — it is not intended as a shopping-list, enabling you to cram for an examination. The guide has three sections.

- **Introduction** — this provides guidance on study and revision, together with advice on approaches and techniques to ensure you answer the examination questions in the best way that you can.
- **Content Guidance** — this section is not intended to be a textbook. It offers guidelines on the main features of the content of Unit 5, together with particular advice on making study more productive.
- **Questions and Answers** — this shows you the sort of questions you can expect in the unit test. Answers are provided; in some cases, distinction is made between responses that might have been given by a grade-A candidate and those typical of a grade-C candidate.

The effective understanding of chemistry requires time. No-one suggests it is an easy subject, but even those who find it difficult can overcome their problems by the proper investment of time.

To understand the chemistry, you have to make links between the various topics. The subject is coherent; it is not a collection of discrete modules. These links only come with experience, which means time spent thinking about chemistry, working with it and solving chemical problems. Time produces fluency with the ideas. If you have that, together with good technique, the examination will look after itself.

The specification

The specification states the chemistry that can be used in the unit tests and describes the format of those tests. This is not necessarily the same as what teachers might choose to teach or what you might choose to learn.

The purpose of this book is to help you with Unit Test 5, but don't forget that what you are doing is learning *chemistry*. The specification can be obtained from Edexcel, either as a printed document or from the web at **www.edexcel.org.uk**.

The unit test

Command terms

Examiners use certain words that require you to respond in a specific way. You must distinguish between these terms and understand exactly what each requires you to do.

- **Define** — give a simple definition without any explanation
- **Identify** — give the name or formula of the substance
- **State** — no explanation is required (nor should you give one)
- **Deduce** — use the information supplied in the question to work out your answer
- **Suggest** — use your knowledge and understanding of similar substances or those with the same functional groups to work out the answer
- **Compare** — make a statement about *both* substances being compared
- **Explain** — use chemical theories or principles to say why a particular property is as it is
- **Predict** — say what you think will happen on the basis of the principles that you have learned

Calculations

You must show your working in order to score full marks. Be careful about significant figures. If a question does not specify the number of significant figures required, give your answer to *three significant figures* or to two decimal places for pH calculations.

Organic formulae

- **Structural formula** — you must give a structure that is unambiguous. For instance, $CH_3CH_2CH_2OH$ is acceptable, but C_3H_7OH could be either propan-1-ol or propan-2-ol and so is not acceptable. If a compound has a double bond, then it should be shown in the structural formula.
- **Full structural formula** — you must show all the *atoms* and all the *bonds*. 'Sticks' instead of hydrogen atoms will lose marks.
- **Shape** — if the molecule or ion is pyramidal, tetrahedral or octahedral you must make sure that your diagram looks three-dimensional. To do this, use wedges and dashes. Draw optical isomers as mirror images of each other. Geometric isomers must be drawn with bond angles of 120°. Make sure that the *bonds go to the correct atoms*, for example the oxygen in an –OH group or the carbon in –CH_3 and –COOH groups.

Points to watch

- **Stable** — if you use this word, you must qualify it; for example: 'stable to heat'; 'the reaction is thermodynamically stable'; 'the reaction is kinetically stable'; or 'a secondary carbocation intermediate is more stable than a primary carbocation'.

- **Reagents** — if you are asked to identify a reagent, you must give its *full* name or formula. Phrases such as 'acidified dichromate(VI)' will not score full marks. You must identify the acid used and give the reagent's full name, for example 'potassium dichromate(VI)'.
- **Conditions** — the word 'reflux' does not imply heating. If heat is needed, you must say so, i.e. 'heat under reflux'. Don't use abbreviations such as 'hur'.
- **Atoms, molecules and ions** — don't use these words randomly. Ionic compounds contain ions, not molecules.
- **Rules** — don't use rules such as Markovnikov or Le Chatelier to *explain*. However, they can be used to predict.
- **Melting and boiling** — when a molecular covalent substance (such as water) is melted or boiled, *covalent* bonds are *not* broken. So melting and boiling points are connected with the type and strength of *intermolecular* forces. When an ionic substance is melted, the ionic bonds are *not* broken — the substance is still ionic. The ions gain enough energy to separate.

Learning to learn

Learning is not instinctive — you have to develop suitable techniques to make good use of your time. In particular, chemistry has peculiar difficulties that need to be understood if your studies are to be effective from the start.

Planning

Busy people do not achieve what they do haphazardly. They plan — so that if they are working they mean to be working, and if they are watching television they have planned to do so. Planning is essential. You must know what you have to do each day and each week and set aside time to do it.

Be realistic in your planning. You cannot work all the time, so you must build in time for recreation and family responsibilities.

Targets

When devising your plan, have a target for each study period. This might be a particular section of the specification, or it might be rearranging of information from text into pictures, or the construction of a flowchart relating all the organic reactions you need to know. Whatever it is, be determined to master your target material before you leave it.

Reading chemistry textbooks

Chemistry textbooks are a valuable resource, not only for finding out the information for your homework but also to help you understand concepts of which you are unsure. They need to be read carefully, with a pen and paper to hand for jotting down things as you go — for example making notes, writing equations, doing calculations and drawing diagrams. Reading and revising are *active* processes which require concentration. Looking vaguely at the pages is a waste of time. In order to become fluent and confident in chemistry, you need to master detail.

Chemical equations

Equations are quantitative, concise and internationally understood.

When you write an equation, check that:
- you have thought of the *type* of reaction occurring — for example, is it neutralisation, addition or disproportionation?
- you have written the correct formulae for all the substances
- your equation balances both for the numbers of atoms of each element and for charge
- you have not written something silly, such as having a strong acid as a product when one of the reactants is an alkali
- you have included *state symbols* in all thermochemical equations and otherwise if they have been asked for

Graphs

Graphs give a lot of information, and they must be understood in detail rather than as a general impression. Take time over them. Note what the axes are, the units, the shape of the graph and what the shape means in chemical terms. Think about what could be calculated from the graph. Note if the graph flattens off and what that means. This is especially important in kinetics.

When drawing a graph, do not join up the points — draw a smooth line (straight or curved) as near as possible to all the points. However, if you are plotting a list, such as the first ionisation energies of the elements, then you do join up the points.

Tables

These are a means of displaying a lot of information. You need to be aware of the table headings and the units of numerical entries. Take time over them. What trends can be seen? How do these relate to chemical properties? Sometimes it can be useful to convert tables of data into graphs. When answering questions, use all the given data.

Diagrams

Diagrams of apparatus should be drawn in section. When you see them, copy them and ask yourself why the apparatus has the features it has. What is the difference between a distillation and a reflux apparatus, for example? When you do practical work, examine each piece of the apparatus closely so that you know both its form and function. Make sure you can draw standard apparatus.

Calculations

Do not take calculations on trust — work through them. First, make certain that you understand the problem, and then that you can follow each step in the solution.

Calculations are not normally structured in A2 as they were in AS. Therefore, you will need to *plan* the procedure for turning the data into an answer.

- Set your calculations out fully, making it clear what you are calculating at each step. Don't round figures up or down during a calculation. Either keep all the numbers on your calculator or write any intermediate answers to four significant figures.
- If you have time, check the accuracy of each step by recalculating it. It is so easy to enter a wrong number into your calculator or to calculate a molar mass incorrectly.
- Finally, check that you have the correct *units* in your answer and that you have given it to an appropriate number of *significant figures* — if in doubt, give it to three.

Notes

Most students keep notes of some sort. Notes can take many forms: they might be permanent or temporary; they might be lists, diagrams or flowcharts. You have to develop your own styles — note the plural. For example, notes that are largely words can often be recast into charts or pictures and this is useful for imprinting the material. The more you rework the material, the clearer it will become.

Whatever form your notes take, they must be organised. Notes that are not indexed or filed properly are useless, as are notes written at enormous length and those written so cryptically that they are unintelligible a month later.

Writing

There is some requirement for extended writing in Unit Test 5. You need to be able to write concisely and accurately. This requires you to marshal your thoughts properly and needs to be practised during your ordinary learning.

For experimental plans, it is a good idea to write your answer as a series of bullet points. There are no marks specifically for 'communication skills', but if you are not able to communicate your ideas clearly and accurately, you will not score full marks. The space available for an answer is a poor guide to the amount that you have to write — handwriting sizes differ hugely, as does the ability to write crisply. Filling the space does not necessarily mean you have answered the question. The mark allocation suggests the number of points to be made, not the amount of writing needed.

Approaching the unit test

The unit test is designed to allow you to show the examiner what you know. Answering questions successfully is not only a matter of knowing the chemistry but is also a matter of technique. Unit Test 5 is a paper with structured questions only, which are answered on the question paper.

Revision

- Start your revision in plenty of time. Make a list of what you need to do, emphasising the topics that you find most difficult — and draw up a detailed revision plan. Work back from the examination date, ideally leaving an entire week free from fresh revision before that date. Be realistic in your revision plan and then add 25% to the timings because everything takes longer than you think.

- When revising, make a note of difficulties and ask your teacher about them. If you do not make these notes, you will forget to ask.
- Make use of past papers. Similar questions are regularly asked, so if you work through as many past papers and answers as possible, you will be in a strong position to obtain a top grade.
- When you use the Question and Answer section of this guide, make a determined effort to write *your* answers *before* looking at the sample answers and examiner's comments.

The exam

Unit Test 5 consists of a structured question paper of duration 1 hour 30 minutes, worth 75 marks. This counts for 30% of the A2 or 15% of the A-level marks.

This unit test examines the content of Unit 5 and some synoptic issues. It also tests your exam technique!

- Read the question. Questions usually change from one examination to the next. A question that looks the same, at a cursory glance, to one that you have seen before usually has significant differences when read carefully. Needless to say, candidates do not receive credit for writing answers to their own questions.
- Be aware of the number of marks available for a question. This is an excellent pointer to the number of things you need to say.
- Do not repeat the question in your answer. We can all see the question. The danger is that you fill up the space available and think that you have answered the question, when in reality some or maybe all of the real points have been ignored.
- Look for words in **bold** in a question and make sure that you have answered the question fully in terms of those words or phrases. For example, if the question asks you to define a **dative covalent bond**, make sure that you explain the meaning of covalent bond as well as dative.
- Questions in Unit Test 5 will often involve substances or situations that are new to you. This is deliberate and is what makes these questions synoptic. Don't be put off by large organic molecules. They are nothing more than a collection of functional groups which, you may assume, react independently of each other.

Unit Test 5 has three assessment objectives:

- AO1 is 'knowledge with understanding' and makes up 20% of the test. You should be able to:
  - recognise, recall and show understanding of specific chemical facts, principles, concepts, practical techniques and terminology
  - draw on existing knowledge to show understanding of the responsible use of chemistry in society
  - select, organise and present information clearly and logically, using specialist vocabulary where appropriate

- AO2 is 'application of knowledge and understanding, analysis, synthesis and evaluation' and makes up 13% of Unit Test 5. You should be able to:
  - describe, explain and interpret phenomena and effects in terms of chemical principles and concepts
  - present arguments and ideas clearly and logically, using specialist vocabulary where appropriate
  - interpret and translate, from one form into another, data presented as continuous prose or in tables, diagrams and graphs
  - carry out calculations
  - apply chemical principles and concepts to unfamiliar situations, including those related to the responsible use of chemistry in society
  - assess the validity of chemical information, experiments, inferences and statements
- AO4 is 'synthesis of knowledge, understanding and skills' and makes up 67% of the test. You should be able to:
  - bring together knowledge, principles and concepts from different areas of chemistry, including experiment and investigation, and apply them in a particular context, expressing ideas clearly and logically and using appropriate specialist vocabulary
  - use chemical skills in contexts which bring together different areas of the subject

Synoptic issues

Much of this unit test will be synoptic assessment, which is the explicit drawing together of knowledge, understanding and skills learned in different parts of the A-level course. In Unit Test 5, this is limited to questions that draw on the whole organic chemistry content of previous units and those that link together different topics within Unit 5.

Content
Guidance

This section is a guide to the content of **Unit 5: Transition Metals, Quantitative Kinetics and Applied Organic Chemistry**. It does not constitute a textbook for Unit 5 material.

The main areas of this unit are:

- Redox equilibria — standard electrode potentials; prediction of the direction of redox reactions
- Transition metal chemistry — electronic configurations and properties of transition metals; bonding and shape of complex ions; deprotonation and ligand exchange reactions; vanadium chemistry
- Organic chemistry — aromatic compounds and reaction mechanisms
- Chemical kinetics — rate equations, rate constants, orders of reaction, rate-determining steps, graphical representation of data
- Further organic chemistry — analysis, including spectra; synthesis; practical techniques; pharmaceuticals; fertilisers; natural esters; polymers (including environmental issues)

Two-thirds of the unit test is synoptic. Therefore, these topics must be studied in conjunction with related topics in earlier units. Of particular importance are oxidation and reduction, shapes of molecules and ions, calculations, kinetics and organic chemistry.

For each part of the specification, you should also consult a standard textbook for more information. Chemistry is a subtle subject, and you need to have a good sense of where the information you are dealing with fits into the larger chemical landscape. This only comes by reading. Remember that the specification tells you only what can be examined in the unit test.

Redox equilibria

Required AS chemistry

Questions set on this topic may require the application of knowledge from Unit 1 (Topic 1.5: Introduction to oxidation and reduction).

Definitions

- **Oxidation** occurs when an atom, molecule or ion *loses* one or more electrons. Its oxidation number increases.
- **Reduction** is when an atom, molecule or ion *gains* one or more electrons. Its oxidation number decreases.
- An **oxidising agent** is a substance that oxidises another substance and is itself reduced. The oxidation number of an element in the oxidising agent decreases.
- A **reducing agent** is a substance that reduces another substance and is itself oxidised. Its oxidation number increases.
- The **oxidation number** of an atom in a compound (or ion) is the charge that it would have if the compound (or ion) were ionic.

Tip Remember **OILRIG** — **O**xidation **I**s **L**oss, **R**eduction **I**s **G**ain.

Oxidation number

The rules for working out oxidation numbers should be applied *in the following order*:

- Rule 1 — the oxidation number of an element in its standard state is zero.
- Rule 2 — a simple monatomic ion has an oxidation number equal to its charge.
- Rule 3 — the sum of the oxidation numbers in a neutral molecule is zero.
- Rule 4 — the sum of the oxidation numbers in an ion add up to the charge on that ion.
- Rule 5 — the oxidation number of hydrogen is +1, except in metal hydrides where it is −1.
- Rule 6 — the oxidation number of oxygen is −2, except in peroxides (e.g. hydrogen peroxide, H_2O_2, where it is −1) or when combined with fluorine, where it is +2.

> **Worked example 1**
> Potassium bromate reacts with potassium bromide in acidic solution according to the equation:
> $$BrO_3^- + 5Br^- + 6H^+ \longrightarrow 3Br_2 + 3H_2O$$
> Determine the oxidation numbers of bromine in BrO_3^-, Br^- and Br_2.

Answer

The oxidation numbers in BrO_3^- add up to -1 (rule 4). Each oxygen is -2 (rule 6); therefore, the three oxygen atoms are $3 \times -2 = -6$. The bromine in BrO_3^- is $+5$, because $+5 + (-6) = -1$.

The oxidation number of bromine in Br^- is -1 (rule 2).

The oxidation number of bromine in Br_2 is zero (rule 1).

Worked example 2

What is the oxidation number of iron in Fe_3O_4?

Answer

The oxidation state of each oxygen is -2 (rule 6); therefore, the four oxygen atoms are $4 \times -2 = -8$. The three iron atoms are $+8$ in total (rule 3). Thus the average oxidation state of each iron atom is $\frac{8}{3} = 2\frac{2}{3}$.

The answer is not a whole number because two of the iron atoms are in the $+3$ state and one is in the $+2$ state.

A2 chemistry

Oxidising agents

Oxidising agents oxidise other substances and are themselves reduced. Oxidation is the *loss* of electrons and so an oxidising agent *removes* electrons from the substance it is oxidising. The oxidation number of an element in the oxidising agent *decreases*.

The half-equation for an oxidising reagent has electrons on the *left-hand* side. The examples shown below have the oxidation numbers written beneath the atoms or ions involved:

$$Cl_2 + 2e^- \longrightarrow 2Cl^-$$
$$2 \times 0 \qquad\qquad 2 \times -1$$

$$Fe^{3+} + e^- \longrightarrow Fe^{2+}$$
$$+3 \qquad\qquad +2$$

Many oxidising agents that contain oxygen need H^+ ions on the left-hand side in the reduction half-equation and produce water on the right — for example, when the dichromate(VI) ion, $Cr_2O_7^{2-}$, acts as an oxidising agent and is reduced to Cr^{3+} ions in acid solution.

$$Cr_2O_7^{2-} + 14H^+ + 6e^- \longrightarrow 2Cr^{3+} + 7H_2O$$
$$2 \times +6 \qquad\qquad\qquad 2 \times +3$$

Total change in oxidation number $= 12$ to $6 = 6$

The *number of electrons* in a half-equation equals the *total* change in oxidation number. The equation must also balance by charge. In the example above, both sides are $+6$.

Sometimes an oxidising agent is used in alkaline solution, in which case H_2O is needed on the left-hand side and OH^- ions are needed on the right-hand side of the half-equation. For example:

$$O_2 + 2H_2O + 4e^- \longrightarrow 4OH^-$$

Each of the oxygen atoms in O_2 changes oxidation number from zero to -2, a change of 4, so there must be four electrons in the half-equation. The stronger the oxidising agent, the larger (more positive or less negative) is its electrode (reduction) potential.

Estimating the concentration of a solution of an oxidising agent

The general method is to add a known volume of the oxidising agent (usually $25\,cm^3$) to an *excess* of acidified potassium iodide and then titrate the liberated iodine with standard sodium thiosulphate solution. Starch is added when the iodine has faded to a pale straw colour, followed by more sodium thiosulphate solution until the blue-black starch–iodine colour disappears.

The equation for the titration reaction is:

$$I_2 + 2Na_2S_2O_3 \longrightarrow 2NaI + Na_2S_4O_6$$

This is an equation that you must know and you must be able to use its stoichiometry to calculate the amount of iodine that reacted with the sodium thiosulphate in the titre.

For example, if the iodine produced required $12.3\,cm^3$ of $0.456\,mol\,dm^{-3}$ sodium thio-sulphate solution, then:

amount (moles) of $Na_2S_2O_3 = 0.456\,mol\,dm^{-3} \times 0.0123\,dm^3 = 0.005609\,mol$
amount (moles) of $I_2 = \frac{1}{2} \times 0.005609 = 0.00280\,mol$

Tip Remember that:

- moles of solute = concentration $(mol\,dm^{-3}) \times$ volume (dm^3)
- volume in $dm^3 = \dfrac{\text{volume in } cm^3}{1000}$

Worked example

$25.0\,cm^3$ of iron(III) chloride solution was added to excess acidified potassium iodide solution. The liberated iodine required $24.2\,cm^3$ of $0.100\,mol\,dm^{-3}$ sodium thiosulphate solution to remove the colour. Calculate the concentration of the iron(III) chloride solution.

Answer

Redox equation: $2FeCl_3 + 2KI \longrightarrow I_2 + 2FeCl_2 + 2KCl$
Titration equation: $I_2 + 2Na_2S_2O_3 \longrightarrow 2NaI + Na_2S_4O_6$

Amount of thiosulphate $= 0.100\,mol\,dm^{-3} \times \dfrac{24.2}{1000}\,dm^3 = 0.00242\,mol$

Amount of iodine $= \frac{1}{2} \times 0.00242 = 0.00121\,mol$ ($\frac{1}{2}$ because 1 mol I_2 reacts with 2 mol $Na_2S_2O_3$)

Amount of $FeCl_3 = 2 \times 0.00121 = 0.00242\,mol$ ($2\times$ because 2 mol $FeCl_3$ produce 1 mol I_2)

Concentration of the $FeCl_3$ solution $= \dfrac{0.00242\,mol}{0.025\,dm^3} = 0.0968\,mol\,dm^{-3}$

Reducing agents

Reducing agents reduce other substances. They do this by *adding* electrons to the other substance. They therefore *lose* electrons, are themselves oxidised and their oxidation number *increases*.

The half-equations for reducing agents have electrons on the *right-hand* side. The examples shown below have the oxidation numbers written beneath the atoms or ions involved:

$$Sn^{2+} \longrightarrow Sn^{4+} + 2e^-$$
$$\phantom{Sn^{2}}+2 +4$$

$$2I^- \longrightarrow I_2 + 2e^-$$
$$2 \times -1 2 \times 0$$

If the reaction takes place in alkaline solution, OH^- ions will probably be needed on the left-hand side of the equation.

$$Cr^{3+} + 7OH^- \longrightarrow CrO_4^- + 3H_2O + 3e^-$$
$$+3 +6$$

Change in oxidation number = 3 to 6 = 3

The *number of electrons* in a half-equation equals the *total* change in oxidation number. The equation must also balance by charge. In the example above, the charge on the left-hand side is $+3 + (-7) = -4$; on the right-hand side it is $-1 + (-3) = -4$.

Estimating the concentration of reducing reagents

Almost all reducing agents reduce potassium manganate(VII) in acid solution. The colour of potassium manganate(VII) is so intense that there is no need to add an indicator.

- Transfer $25.0\,cm^3$ of the solution of the reducing agent from a pipette into a conical flask.
- Add approximately $25\,cm^3$ of dilute sulphuric acid.
- Rinse a burette with water and then with some of a standard solution of potassium manganate(VII).
- Add the potassium manganate(VII) solution from the burette until a faint, permanent, pink colour is obtained.
- Repeat until two consistent titres are obtained and find the average of their values.

Worked example

$25.0\,cm^3$ of a solution of tin(II) chloride was added to excess dilute sulphuric acid and titrated with $0.0202\,mol\,dm^{-3}$ potassium manganate(VII) solution. The average titre was $26.2\,cm^3$. Calculate the concentration of the tin(II) chloride solution.

Answer

Redox equation: $5Sn^{2+} + 2MnO_4^- + 16H^+ \longrightarrow 5Sn^{4+} + 2Mn^{2+} + 8H_2O$

Amount of MnO_4^- = 0.0202 mol dm^{-3} × $\frac{26.2}{1000}$ dm^3 = 0.000529 mol

Amount of Sn^{2+} = 0.000529 × $\frac{5}{2}$ = 0.00132 mol

Concentration of $SnCl_2$ = $\frac{0.00132 \text{ mol}}{0.025 \text{ dm}^3}$ = 0.0529 mol dm^{-3}

Standard electrode potentials

These are normally written as *reduction* potentials, with electrons on the left-hand side and a reversible symbol rather than an arrow.

Standard electrode potential is defined as the potential of the half-cell measured against a standard hydrogen electrode under standard conditions, which are:
- all solutions of concentration 1 mol dm^{-3}
- all gases at 1 atmosphere pressure
- a temperature of 298 K

For zinc, it is the potential of a zinc rod dipping into a 1.0 mol dm^{-3} solution of Zn^{2+} ions at 298 K. The equation is:

$$Zn^{2+}(aq) + 2e^- \rightleftharpoons Zn(s)$$

For chlorine, it is the potential of chlorine gas, at 1 atm pressure, bubbled over a platinum electrode dipping into a 1.0 mol dm^{-3} solution of Cl$^-$ ions at 298 K. The equation is:

$$Cl_2(g) + 2e^- \rightleftharpoons 2Cl^-(aq)$$

For the Fe^{3+}/Fe^{2+} half-cell, it is the potential when a platinum electrode is placed into a solution of concentration 1.0 mol dm^{-3} in *both* Fe^{3+} and Fe^{2+} ions. The equation is:

$$Fe^{3+}(aq) + e^- \rightleftharpoons Fe^{2+}(aq)$$

Note that:
- a standard hydrogen electrode has to be used as only potential *differences* can be measured
- the value of the standard hydrogen electrode is defined as zero
- all soluble substances, whether they are on the left or the right of the equation, must be at a concentration of 1.0 mol dm^{-3}, if the *standard* potential is being measured

Writing overall redox equations

Questions will often provide the necessary reduction half-equations and ask the candidate to write an overall equation. This is done in four steps:

Step 1: Look at the overall reaction and identify the *reactants* in the two half-equations. One reactant (the oxidising agent) will be on the left-hand side of one half-equation and the other reactant (the reducing agent) will be on the right-hand side of the other half-equation.

Step 2: Reverse the equation that has the reactant on the *right*.

Step 3: Multiply one or both equations so that both now have the same number of electrons. One equation will still have the electrons on the left and the other will have them on the right.

Step 4: Add the two equations. *Cancel* the electrons, as there will be the same number on each side of the equation.

Worked example

Ethanedioate ions, $C_2O_4^{2-}$, are oxidised by manganate(VII) ions, MnO_4^-, in acid solution. The two reduction half-equations are:

$$2CO_2 + 2e^- \rightleftharpoons C_2O_4^{2-}$$
$$MnO_4^- + 8H^+ + 5e^- \rightleftharpoons Mn^{2+} + 4H_2O$$

Answer

Step 1: the reactants are MnO_4^- and $C_2O_4^{2-}$

Step 2: reverse the first equation:

$$C_2O_4^{2-} \rightleftharpoons 2CO_2 + 2e^-$$

Step 3: multiply the reversed first equation by 5 and the second equation by 2:

$$5C_2O_4^{2-} \rightleftharpoons 10CO_2 + 10e^-$$
$$2MnO_4^- + 16H^+ + 10e^- \rightleftharpoons 2Mn^{2+} + 8H_2O$$

Note that one equation now has the electrons on the right and the other still has them on the left.

Step 4: add to give the overall equation:

$$5C_2O_4^{2-} + 2MnO_4^- + 16H^+ \longrightarrow 10CO_2 + 2Mn^{2+} + 8H_2O$$

Predicting the direction of redox reactions

There are two ways of predicting whether or not a redox reaction will take place, based on electrode potential data.

Method 1

This method uses the overall equation. It is the best method if you are also asked to deduce the overall equation. The method is similar to that for writing overall redox equations but the values of the electrode potentials are also used.

Using the same example as above, and given the two electrode potential half-equations:

$$2CO_2 + 2e^- \rightleftharpoons C_2O_4^{2-} \qquad E^\ominus = -0.49 \text{ V}$$
$$MnO_4^- + 8H^+ + 5e^- \rightleftharpoons Mn^{2+} + 4H_2O \qquad E^\ominus = +1.52 \text{ V}$$

Step 1: As before, identify the reactants ($C_2O_4^{2-}$ and MnO_4^-).

Step 2: Reverse the top equation. *You must change the sign of $E^\ominus$ in the reversed equation:*

$$C_2O_4^{2-} \rightleftharpoons 2CO_2 + 2e^- \qquad E^\ominus = +0.49 \text{ V}$$

Step 3: Multiply both equations by whole numbers so that both have the same number of electrons. *Do not multiply the $E^\ominus$ values.*

Step 4: Add the two equations and *add the two $E^\ominus$ values* to give $E^\ominus_{cell}$.

$$5C_2O_4^{2-} \rightleftharpoons 10CO_2 + 10e^- \qquad\qquad E^\ominus = +0.49 \text{ V}$$

$$2MnO_4^- + 16H^+ + 10e^- \rightleftharpoons 2Mn^{2+} + 8H_2O \qquad\qquad E^\ominus = +1.52 \text{ V}$$

$$5C_2O_4^{2-} + 2MnO_4^- + 16H^+ \longrightarrow 10CO_2 + 2Mn^{2+} + 8H_2O$$
$$E^\ominus_{cell} = +0.49 + 1.52 = +2.01 \text{ V}$$

As this is a *positive* number, the reaction should take place from left to right. If adding gives a negative value for $E^\ominus_{cell}$, the reaction will go from right to left.

Method 2

This method uses the rule:

$\quad E^\ominus_{cell} = E^\ominus$ of oxidising agent $- E^\ominus$ of reducing agent

Step 1: Identify the oxidising agent. Remember that the oxidising agent will be reduced and so will be on the left of a standard electrode (reduction) potential equation.

Step 2: Identify the reducing agent. The reducing agent will be oxidised and so will be on the right of a standard electrode (reduction) potential.

Step 3: Calculate $E^\ominus_{cell} = E^\ominus$ of oxidising agent $- E^\ominus$ of reducing agent.

Tip Remember that both the oxidising agent and the reducing agent must be the *reactants* stated in the question. In the example below they are dichromate(VI) ions and chloride ions, and *not* the chlorine molecule.

As an example of this method, the following data are used to decide if dichromate(VI) ions will react with chloride ions:

$$Cr_2O_7^{2-} + 6e^- + 14H^+ \rightleftharpoons 2Cr^{3+} + 7H_2O \quad E^\ominus = +1.33 \text{ V}$$
$$Cl_2 + 2e^- \rightleftharpoons 2Cl^- \qquad\qquad\qquad\qquad E^\ominus = +1.36 \text{ V}$$

The reactants are $Cr_2O_7^{2-}$ and Cl^-.

Step 1: The oxidising agent is $Cr_2O_7^{2-}$. It would be reduced to Cr^{3+}.
Step 2: The reducing agent is Cl^-. It would be oxidised to Cl_2.
Step 3: $E^\ominus_{cell} = +1.33 - (+1.36) = -0.03 \text{ V}$
$\quad\quad E^\ominus_{cell}$ is *negative* and so the reaction will *not* take place.

Worked example (using both methods)

Will manganate(VI) ions, MnO_4^{2-}, disproportionate in acid solution to manganate(VII) ions, MnO_4^-, and manganese(IV) oxide? If so, write the overall equation.

$$MnO_4^- + e^- \rightleftharpoons MnO_4^{2-} \qquad\qquad E^\ominus = +0.56 \text{ V}$$
$$MnO_4^{2-} + 4H^+ + 2e^- \rightleftharpoons MnO_2 + 2H_2O \qquad E^\ominus = +1.75 \text{ V}$$

Answer using method 1

As it is a disproportionation reaction, both reactants are the same substance — in this example, MnO_4^{2-} ions.

Reverse the first equation, double it and add it to the second equation.

$$2MnO_4^{2-} \rightleftharpoons 2MnO_4^- + 2e^- \qquad\qquad E^\ominus = -0.56 \text{ V}$$
$$MnO_4^{2-} + 4H^+ + 2e^- \rightleftharpoons MnO_2 + 2H_2O \qquad E^\ominus = +1.75 \text{ V}$$

The equation is:

$$3MnO_4^{2-} + 4H^+ \longrightarrow 2MnO_4^- + MnO_2 + 2H_2O \qquad E^\ominus_{cell} = -0.56 + 1.75 = +1.19 \text{ V}$$

As $E^\ominus_{cell}$ is positive, the reaction will take place.

Answer using method 2

The oxidising agent is manganate(VI), which is reduced to MnO_2. The reducing agent is also manganate(VI), which is oxidised to MnO_4^-.

$$E^\ominus_{cell} = +1.75 - (+0.56) = +1.19 \text{ V}$$

As the value of $E^\ominus_{cell}$ is positive, the disproportionation reaction should take place. To find the equation, use the same procedure as in method 1.

Note: a disproportionation reaction is where one element in a species is simultaneously oxidised and reduced. Therefore, the element must have three oxidation states — the starting value, one higher than the starting value and one lower. In the example above, manganese starts in the +6 state, is oxidised to the +7 state and simultaneously reduced to the +4 state.

Non-standard conditions

If the conditions are not standard, that is, when one of the reactants is not at a concentration of 1 mol dm^{-3} or, in particular, when one of the products is insoluble, the prediction from the value of $E^\ominus_{cell}$ may not be valid.

Under standard conditions, with a concentration of Cu^{2+} equal to 1 mol dm^{-3}, copper(II) ions will oxidise iodide ions, even though $E^\ominus_{cell}$ for the reaction is negative.

$$2Cu^{2+}(aq) + 2I^-(aq) \rightleftharpoons 2Cu^+(aq) + I_2(aq) \qquad E^\ominus_{cell} = -0.39 \text{ V}$$

This is because copper(I) iodide is insoluble, the equilibrium is driven to the right and the overall equation becomes:

$$2Cu^{2+}(aq) + 4I^-(aq) \longrightarrow 2CuI(s) + I_2(aq)$$

Some reactions with a positive value of $E^\ominus_{cell}$ may not occur because the activation energy is too high, making the reaction so slow that it is not observed.

Corrosion

Iron is the most commonly used metal, because it is the cheapest and it is strong. However, it corrodes in damp air. Corrosion is a redox process. Acting as an anode, the iron atoms lose electrons.

$$Fe(s) \longrightarrow Fe^{2+} + 2e^- \qquad E^\ominus = +0.44 \text{ V}$$

At the surface of the water droplet or at stress points on the metal surface (the cathode), dissolved oxygen is reduced.

$$\tfrac{1}{2}O_2(aq) + H_2O + 2e^- \longrightarrow 2OH^-(aq) \qquad E^\ominus = +0.40 \text{ V}$$

As $E^{\ominus}_{cell}$ for this process is +0.84 V, it does occur — the iron rusts in the presence of an aqueous layer. The positive Fe^{2+} ions are attracted to the negative OH^- ions and a precipitate of iron(II) hydroxide forms.

$$Fe^{2+}(aq) + 2OH^-(aq) \longrightarrow Fe(OH)_2(s)$$

This is then oxidised by more dissolved oxygen to hydrated iron(III) oxide, or rust.

Prevention of corrosion

For corrosion to take place, water containing dissolved oxygen must be in contact with the iron. Corrosion can be prevented by placing a physical barrier between the iron and the water. This can be done in several ways:

- painting the surface of the iron
- plating a metal that does not corrode onto the surface of the iron, for example chrome plating, tin plating (as in food tins) or plating a layer of silver on a layer of nickel over the iron (electroplated nickel silver)
- alloying the iron with a metal that forms a protective layer of oxide — stainless steel is an example, where the iron is mixed with chromium
- coating the iron with oil — WD40 is denser than water, so the water floats on it and cannot come into contact with the iron

Another method of prevention is to coat the iron with a sacrificial metal, which is then preferentially oxidised. **Galvanising**, in which the iron is coated with a layer of zinc, is an example. $E^{\ominus}$ for zinc is +0.76 V, which is more positive than $E^{\ominus}$ for iron, so the zinc corrodes first.

Dissolved ionic substances, such as salt, increase the rate of corrosion because they raise the electrical conductivity of the aqueous layer.

Storage cells

There are two necessary conditions for storage cells:

- The reactions must be *reversible redox* reactions. Electricity is *produced* in the discharge reaction but the reaction can be reversed by passing an electric current through the cell.
- The redox products in both the discharge and the charging reactions must be *insoluble*, so that they stick to the surface of the electrodes.

The following reactions take place in the lead/acid (car) battery during discharge.

- At the negative anode (oxidation):
  $$Pb(s) + SO_4^{2-}(aq) \longrightarrow PbSO_4(s) + 2e^- \qquad E^{\ominus} = +0.36 \text{ V}$$
- At the positive cathode (reduction):
  $$PbO_2(s) + 2H_2SO_4(aq) + 2e^- \longrightarrow PbSO_4(s) + SO_4^{2-}(aq) + 2H_2O(l) \qquad E^{\ominus} = +1.69 \text{ V}$$
- Adding gives the overall equation:
  $$Pb(s) + PbO_2(s) + 2H_2SO_4(aq) \longrightarrow 2PbSO_4(s) + 2H_2O \qquad E^{\ominus}_{cell} = +2.05 \text{ V}$$

If a voltage greater than 2.05 V is applied, the reaction is forced in the opposite direction and the cell is recharged.

Transition metal chemistry

Here are some important definitions:

- **d-block elements** are those in which the last electron has gone into a d-orbital.
- A **transition element** has partially filled d-orbitals in its atoms or in one or more of its cations. Transition elements are all d-block elements. All are metals; most are physically strong and have high melting points.
- A **ligand** is a molecule or negative ion that forms a dative bond with a d-block cation.
- The **coordination number** is the number of ligands around a central d-block cation.
- A **dative (coordinate) bond** is formed when two atoms share a pair of electrons, both of which are supplied by one atom.

Tip On defining a d-block element, do not say 'outermost electrons are in d-orbitals', or 'the highest energy electron is in a d-orbital', because neither is true.

Electron configuration

The electronic configurations of the d-block elements are shown in the table below.

Element		3d	4s
Sc	$[Ar]3d^14s^2$	↑ | | | |	↑↓
Ti	$[Ar]3d^24s^2$	↑ | ↑ | | |	↑↓
V	$[Ar]3d^34s^2$	↑ | ↑ | ↑ | |	↑↓
Cr	$[Ar]3d^54s^1$	↑ | ↑ | ↑ | ↑ | ↑	↑
Mn	$[Ar]3d^54s^2$	↑ | ↑ | ↑ | ↑ | ↑	↑↓
Fe	$[Ar]3d^64s^2$	↑↓ | ↑ | ↑ | ↑ | ↑	↑↓
Co	$[Ar]3d^74s^2$	↑↓ | ↑↓ | ↑ | ↑ | ↑	↑↓
Ni	$[Ar]3d^84s^2$	↑↓ | ↑↓ | ↑↓ | ↑ | ↑	↑↓
Cu	$[Ar]3d^{10}4s^1$	↑↓ | ↑↓ | ↑↓ | ↑↓ | ↑↓	↑
Zn	$[Ar]3d^{10}4s^2$	↑↓ | ↑↓ | ↑↓ | ↑↓ | ↑↓	↑↓

Note: [Ar] is short for $1s^22s^22p^63s^23p^6$.

All the elements have the configuration $[Ar]3d^x4s^2$, except chromium which is $[Ar]3d^54s^1$ and copper which is $[Ar]3d^{10}4s^1$. The difference is caused by the extra stability of a half-filled or fully filled orbital type, which makes it energetically preferable for an electron to move out of the $4s$ orbital into a $3d$ orbital. An atom of iron has six $3d$ electrons because it is the sixth d-block element. When an element forms a cation (positive ion), it first loses its $4s$ electrons. The electronic configurations of atomic iron, the Fe^{2+} ion and the Fe^{3+} ion are:

Element		3d	4s
Fe	$[Ar]3d^64s^2$	↑↓ ↑ ↑ ↑ ↑	↑↓
Fe^{2+}	$[Ar]3d^6$	↑↓ ↑ ↑ ↑ ↑	
Fe^{3+}	$[Ar]3d^5$	↑ ↑ ↑ ↑ ↑	

Properties of transition elements

Variable oxidation state

Transition elements have several different oxidation states. The common oxidation states of the d-block metals are shown in the table below.

Sc	Ti	V	Cr	Mn	Fe	Co	Ni	Cu	Zn
								+1	
		+2	+2	+2	+2	+2	+2	+2	+2
+3	+3	+3	+3		+3	+3			
	+4	+4		+4					
		+5							
			+6	+6					
				+7					

- Scandium forms only Sc^{3+} ions, which have no d-electrons; zinc forms only Zn^{2+} ions which have ten d-electrons. Therefore, neither is classified as a transition element.
- Chromium can be: Cr^{2+}, as in $CrCl_2$; Cr^{3+}, as in $Cr_2(SO_4)_3$; in the +6 state, as in K_2CrO_4 and $K_2Cr_2O_7$.
- Iron can be: Fe^{2+}, as in $FeSO_4$; Fe^{3+}, as in $FeCl_3$.
- Copper can be: Cu^+, as in $CuCl$ and Cu_2O; Cu^{2+}, as in $CuSO_4$ and CuO.

Transition metals can form stable cations with different charges because the successive ionisation energies increase steadily. For example, the extra energy required to remove a third electron from Fe^{2+} is compensated for by the *extra hydration enthalpy* of the 3+ ion compared with the 2+ ion. The third ionisation energy of iron ($Fe^{2+}(g) \longrightarrow Fe^{3+}(g) + e^-$) is $+2960\ kJ\ mol^{-1}$, but the hydration energy of the $Fe^{3+}(g)$ ion ($Fe^{3+}(g) + aq \longrightarrow Fe^{3+}(aq)$) is $2920\ kJ\ mol^{-1}$ *more exothermic* than that of the $Fe^{2+}(g)$ ion.

With calcium, an *s*-block element, the third ionisation energy is $+4940\ kJ\ mol^{-1}$, which is not compensated for by the extra hydration enthalpy. The third ionisation energy is much higher because the third electron in calcium is removed from an inner $3p$ shell. A transition metal such as chromium can also form oxo-anions, such as CrO_4^{2-}, because it uses all its $4s$ and $3d$ electrons in forming six covalent bonds (4σ and 2π) with oxygen. It accepts six electrons to give the configuration $3d^{10}4s^2$.

Formation of complex ions

- All transition metal ions form complexes. A complex ion is formed when a number of ligands (usually four or six) bond to a central metal ion. The bonding is dative covalent with a lone pair of electrons on the ligand forming a bond with empty $3d$, $4s$ and $4p$ orbitals in the metal ion.
- Ligands can be neutral molecules, such as H_2O and NH_3, or negative ions, such as Cl^- and CN^-. Some ligands, for instance in haemoglobin, are complicated molecules.
- All transition metals form hexaaqua hydrated ions, such as $[Cr(H_2O)_6]^{3+}$.
- Zinc, a *d*-block metal, forms the $[Zn(H_2O)_4]^{2+}$ ion.
- In aqua complexes, the bonding between the oxygen atoms and the central metal ion is dative covalent and the bonding within the water molecule is covalent.
- All six-coordinate complexes are *octahedral* with 90° bond angles because there are six pairs of bonding electrons around the metal ion and these six *bond pairs* repel each other to a position of *maximum separation*.

Tip Do not say that the *atoms* or the *bonds* repel. It is the *bond pairs* of electrons that repel.

- Solutions of the hexaaqua ions of highly charged, small, 3+ ions such as Cr^{3+} are acidic, because of their polarising power.

$$[Cr(H_2O)_6]^{3+} + H_2O \longrightarrow [Cr(H_2O)_5OH]^{2+} + H_3O^+$$

  Acid 1   Base 2   Conjugate base 1   Conjugate acid 2

  This is an example of deprotonation. Hydrated iron(III) ions are acidic for the same reason.
- Fe^{2+} and Fe^{3+} ions form complexes with cyanide ions, $[Fe(CN)_6]^{4-}$ and $[Fe(CN)_6]^{3-}$.
- Cu^{2+} ions form a complex with ammonia, $[Cu(NH_3)_4(H_2O)_2]^{2+}$.
- Chloride ions are much larger than water molecules, so there is a maximum of four Cl^- ions around a transition metal ion in chloro-complexes. For example, the complexes of copper(I) and copper(II) with chloride ions have the formulae $[CuCl_2]^-$ and $[CuCl_4]^{2-}$.

Coloured complex ions

The ligands around the central ion split the d-orbitals into a group of three of lower energy and a group of two of higher energy. When light is shone into a solution of a complex ion, the ion absorbs light energy and an electron is promoted to the upper of the two split d-levels. If both red light and yellow light are absorbed, the ion appears blue.

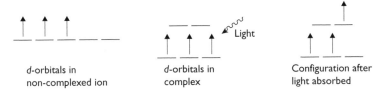

| d-orbitals in non-complexed ion | d-orbitals in complex | Configuration after light absorbed |

- Sc^{3+} and Ti^{4+} ions have no d-electrons. Cu^+ and Zn^{2+} ions have a full set of 10 d-electrons. Therefore, no d–d transitions are possible. Hence, these ions are colourless.
- $[Cr(H_2O)_6]^{2+}$ is blue; $[Cr(H_2O)_6]^{3+}$ is green.
- $[Fe(H_2O)_6]^{2+}$ is green; $[Fe(H_2O)_6]^{3+}$ is amethyst (solutions appear yellow-brown due to deprotonation of the hydrated ion).
- $[Cu(H_2O)_6]^{2+}$ is pale blue; $[Cu(NH_3)_4(H_2O)_2]^{2+}$ is dark blue.

Catalytic activity

Transition metals and their compounds are often excellent catalysts. The metals use their d-orbitals to provide active sites on their surfaces to which reactants bond. For example, nickel is the catalyst for the addition of hydrogen to alkenes and iron is used in the Haber process, catalysing the reaction:

$$N_2 + 3H_2 \rightleftharpoons 2NH_3$$

Compounds of transition metals can change oxidation state and this is made use of industrially. Vanadium(V) oxide is the catalyst in the manufacture of sulphuric acid, and catalyses the reaction:

$$2SO_2 + O_2 \rightleftharpoons 2SO_3$$

It can do this because of the variable valency of vanadium. The mechanism is:

Step 1: $2SO_2 + 2V_2O_5 \longrightarrow 2SO_3 + 4VO_2$
Step 2: $4VO_2 + O_2 \longrightarrow 2V_2O_5$
Overall: $2SO_2 + O_2 \longrightarrow 2SO_3$

Fe^{3+} ions catalyse the oxidation of iodide ions by persulphate ions, $S_2O_8^{2-}$. The mechanism is:

Step 1: $2Fe^{3+}(aq) + 2I^-(aq) \longrightarrow 2Fe^{2+}(aq) + I_2(s)$
Step 2: $2Fe^{2+}(aq) + S_2O_8^{2-}(aq) \longrightarrow 2Fe^{3+}(aq) + 2SO_4^{2-}(aq)$
Overall: $2I^-(aq) + S_2O_8^{2-}(aq) \longrightarrow I_2(s) + 2SO_4^{2-}(aq)$

Reactions of d-block metal compounds

Reactions with aqueous sodium hydroxide

All the hydrated ions are **deprotonated** by $OH^-(aq)$ ions. A precipitate of the neutral hydrated hydroxide is formed.

$$[M(H_2O)_6]^{2+}(aq) + 2OH^-(aq) \longrightarrow [M(H_2O)_4(OH)_2](s) + 2H_2O(l)$$
$$[M(H_2O)_6]^{3+}(aq) + 3OH^-(aq) \longrightarrow [M(H_2O)_3(OH)_3](s) + 3H_2O(l)$$

where M stands for any transition metal cation.

Note that the number of hydroxide ions on the left-hand side and the number of water molecules on the right-hand side of the equation are equal to the charge on the transition metal ion.

The colour changes are shown in the table below.

Complex	Colour of complex	Hydroxide	Comment
$[Cr(H_2O)_6]^{3+}$	Green solution	Green precipitate	—
$[Mn(H_2O)_6]^{2+}$	Pale pink solution	Sandy precipitate which darkens in air	Manganese is oxidised to the +4 state
$[Fe(H_2O)_6]^{2+}$	Pale green solution	Green precipitate which goes brown in air	Iron is oxidised to the +3 state
$[Fe(H_2O)_6]^{3+}$	Yellow solution	Red-brown precipitate	—
$[Co(H_2O)_6]^{2+}$	Pink solution	Red precipitate which goes blue on standing	Hydrated hydroxide loses its four water molecules
$[Ni(H_2O)_6]^{2+}$	Green solution	Pale green precipitate	—
$[Cu(H_2O)_6]^{2+}$	Blue solution	Blue precipitate	—
$[Zn(H_2O)_4]^{2+}$	Colourless solution	White precipitate	—

Reactions with excess aqueous sodium hydroxide

On adding excess sodium hydroxide, amphoteric hydroxides deprotonate further; for example, chromium and zinc hydroxides.

$$[Cr(H_2O)_3(OH)_3] + 3OH^- \longrightarrow [Cr(OH)_6]^{3-} + 3H_2O$$

$[Cr(OH)_6]^{3-}$ is dark green.

$$[Zn(H_2O)_2(OH)_2] + 2OH^- \longrightarrow [Zn(OH)_4]^{2-} + 2H_2O$$

$[Zn(OH)_4]^{2-}$ is colourless.

Aluminium, although not a transition metal, is also amphoteric. Addition of sodium hydroxide to its hexaaqua ion produces a white precipitate of $[Al(H_2O)_3(OH)_3]$, which reacts with excess sodium hydroxide to form a colourless solution of the $[Al(OH)_6]^{3-}$ ion.

Reactions with aqueous ammonia

Ammonia is a base and a ligand. When ammonia solution is added to a solution of a transition metal salt, the hydrated metal ion is deprotonated, as with sodium hydroxide solution, giving the same coloured precipitates. For example:

$$[Fe(H_2O)_6]^{2+} + 2NH_3 \longrightarrow [Fe(H_2O)_4(OH)_2] + 2NH_4^+$$
$$[Fe(H_2O)_6]^{3+} + 3NH_3 \longrightarrow [Fe(H_2O)_3(OH)_3] + 3NH_4^+$$

However, excess ammonia results in **ligand exchange** with nickel, copper and zinc.

- $[Ni(H_2O)_4(OH)_2] + 4NH_3 \longrightarrow [Ni(NH_3)_4(H_2O)_2]^{2+} + 2OH^- + 2H_2O$
  $[Ni(NH_3)_4(H_2O)_2]^{2+}$ is pale blue.

- $[Cu(H_2O)_4(OH)_2] + 4NH_3 \longrightarrow [Cu(NH_3)_4(H_2O)_2]^{2+} + 2OH^- + 2H_2O$
  $[Cu(NH_3)_4(H_2O)_2]^{2+}$ is dark blue.
- $[Zn(H_2O)_2(OH)_2] + 4NH_3 \longrightarrow [Zn(NH_3)_4]^{2+} + 2OH^- + 2H_2O$
  $[Zn(NH_3)_4]^{2+}$ is colourless.

Vanadium chemistry

Oxidation states

There are four oxidation states of vanadium, each with a different colour.

Oxidation state	Formula	Colour
+2	V^{2+}	Lavender
+3	V^{3+}	Green
+4	VO^{2+}	Blue
+5	VO_2^+	Yellow

VO_2^+ is in equilibrium with the colourless VO_3^- ion.

$$VO_3^- + 2H^+ \rightleftharpoons VO_2^+ + H_2O$$

Redox reactions

Reduction by zinc and hydrochloric acid

The full range of colours is seen when vanadium(V) is reduced by zinc and dilute hydrochloric acid — yellow (+5) to green (a mixture of +5 and +4), through blue (+4) and green (+3) to lavender (+2).

Standard reduction potentials

Oxidation state change	Equation	$E^\ominus$/V
+5 $\longrightarrow$ +4	$VO_2^+ + 2H^+ + e^- \rightleftharpoons VO^{2+} + H_2O$	+1.0 V
+4 $\longrightarrow$ +3	$VO^{2+} + 2H^+ + e^- \rightleftharpoons V^{3+} + H_2O$	+0.3 V
+3 $\longrightarrow$ +2	$V^{3+} + e^- \rightleftharpoons V^{2+}$	−0.3 V

Partial reduction

- A reducing agent will reduce +5 to +4 but no further, if its standard reduction potential is between +0.3 and +1.0 V.
- A reducing agent will reduce +5 to +3 but not to +2, if its standard reduction potential is between −0.3 V and +0.3 V.
- A reducing agent will reduce +5 to +2, if its standard reduction potential is less than −0.3 V.

Worked example

How far will a solution of Fe^{2+} ions reduce a solution of VO_2^+?

$$Fe^{3+} + e^- \rightleftharpoons Fe^{2+} \quad E^\ominus = +0.77 \text{ V}$$

Answer

+0.77 V is between +0.3 V and +1.0 V, and so Fe^{2+} should reduce vanadium(V) to vanadium(IV) and no further. To prove this, reverse the Fe^{3+}/Fe^{2+} equation and add it to the one for vanadium changing oxidation state from +5 to +4.

$$Fe^{2+} + VO_2^+ + 2H^+ \rightleftharpoons Fe^{3+} + VO^{2+} + H_2O \qquad E^{\ominus}_{cell} = +1.0 + (-0.77) = +0.23 \text{ V}$$

As $E^{\ominus}_{cell}$ is positive, the reaction will occur. Therefore, Fe^{2+} will reduce vanadium +5 to the +4 state. (See pages 18–19 for how to work out the overall redox equation and its feasibility.)

However, reversing the Fe^{3+}/Fe^{2+} equation and adding it to the one for vanadium +4 to +3 gives:

$$Fe^{2+} + VO^{2+} + 2H^+ \rightleftharpoons Fe^{3+} + V^{3+} + H_2O \qquad E^{\ominus}_{cell} = +0.3 + (-0.77) = -0.47 \text{ V}$$

$E^{\ominus}_{cell}$ is negative, so the reaction will not occur. Fe^{2+} ions will not reduce the solution to the +3 state.

Partial oxidation

- An oxidising agent will oxidise vanadium in the +3 state to +4 and no further, if its standard electrode potential is between +0.3 V and +1.0 V.
- An oxidising agent will oxidise vanadium in the +3 or +4 state to the +5 state, if its standard reduction potential is greater than +1.0 V.

The value for the Fe^{3+}/Fe^{2+} equation is +0.77 V, which is between +0.3 and +1.0 V. Therefore, Fe^{3+} oxidises V^{3+} to the +4 state but no further. This is shown by:

$$Fe^{3+} + V^{3+} + H_2O \rightleftharpoons Fe^{2+} + VO^{2+} + 2H^+ \qquad E^{\ominus}_{cell} = +0.77 - 0.30 = +0.47 \text{ V}$$

$E^{\ominus}_{cell}$ is positive and so Fe^{3+} ions oxidise vanadium(III) to vanadium(IV). However:

$$Fe^{3+} + VO^{2+} + H_2O \rightleftharpoons Fe^{2+} + VO_2^+ + 2H^+ \qquad E^{\ominus}_{cell} = +0.77 - 1.00 = -0.33 \text{ V}$$

In this case, $E^{\ominus}_{cell}$ is negative, so Fe^{3+} ions do not oxidise vanadium(IV) to vanadium(V).

Chlorine oxidises vanadium(III) up to the +5 state, because $E^{\ominus}_{cell}$ is positive.

$$Cl_2 + 2e^- \rightleftharpoons 2Cl^- \qquad\qquad E^{\ominus} = +1.36 \text{ V}$$
$$\tfrac{1}{2}Cl_2 + VO^{2+} + H_2O \rightleftharpoons Cl^- + VO_2^+ + 2H^+ \qquad E^{\ominus}_{cell} = +1.36 - 1.00 = +0.36 \text{ V}$$

Tip Do not confuse VO_2^+ with VO^{2+}. The first has vanadium in the +5 state and the latter in the +4 state.

Reactions to know

Deprotonation

In deprotonation reactions, one or more H^+ ions are removed from water ligands. Deprotonation can be due to the solvent water, which is a very weak base. Therefore, this reaction only happens noticeably with 3+ cation complexes and only one H^+ is removed in an equilibrium reaction.

$$[Fe(H_2O)_6]^{3+} + H_2O \rightleftharpoons [Fe(H_2O)_5(OH)]^{2+} + H_3O^+$$

With stronger bases, such as OH^- ions or ammonia, H^+ ions are removed and the complex becomes neutral and insoluble. This happens with both the 2+ and 3+ cation complexes.

$$[Fe(H_2O)_6]^{3+} + 3OH^- \longrightarrow [Fe(H_2O)_3(OH)_3] + 3H_2O$$

A strong acid, such as dilute sulphuric, reacts with the precipitated hydroxide and re-forms a solution of the hexaaqua complex.

$$[Fe(H_2O)_3(OH)_3] + 3H^+ \longrightarrow [Fe(H_2O)_6]^{3+}$$

Ligand exchange

If cyanide ions are added to hexaaqua iron(III) ions, ligand exchange takes place.

$$[Fe(H_2O)_6]^{3+} + 6CN^- \longrightarrow [Fe(CN)_6]^{3-} + 6H_2O$$

If excess ammonia solution is added to precipitates of the hydroxides of copper(II), zinc, nickel, cobalt or silver, ligand exchange takes place, forming a solution of the ammonia complex of the *d*-block ion.

$$[Cu(H_2O)_4(OH)_2] + 4NH_3 \longrightarrow [Cu(NH_3)_4(H_2O)_2]^{2+} + 2OH^- + 2H_2O$$
$$[Zn(H_2O)_2(OH)_2] + 4NH_3 \longrightarrow [Zn(NH_3)_4]^{2+} + 2OH^- + 2H_2O$$

Redox

You must know the ionic half-equations for the reduction of manganate(VII) ions and chromate(VI) ions and how to use them to find the overall redox equation (see page 18).

The two half-equations are:

$$MnO_4^-(aq) + 8H^+(aq) + 5e^- \rightleftharpoons Mn^{2+}(aq) + 4H_2O(l)$$
$$Cr_2O_7^{2-}(aq) + 14H^+ + 6e^- \rightleftharpoons 2Cr^{3+}(aq) + 7H_2O(l)$$

Catalysed reactions

You need to know the following examples of reactions that are catalysed by transition metals or their compounds.

Reaction	Equation	Catalyst
Alkene + hydrogen	$H_2C=CH_2 + H_2 \rightleftharpoons CH_3CH_3$	Nickel or platinum
Contact process	$2SO_2 + O_2 \rightleftharpoons 2SO_3$	Vanadium(V) oxide
Haber process	$N_2 + 3H_2 \rightleftharpoons 2NH_3$	Iron
Oxidation of ammonia in the manufacture of nitric acid	$4NH_3 + 5O_2 \longrightarrow 4NO + 6H_2O$	Platinum

Organic chemistry — aromatic compounds and reaction mechanisms

Definitions

- An **addition reaction** occurs when two substances combine to form a single substance. For example:

  $$H_2C=CH_2 + Br_2 \longrightarrow CH_2BrCH_2Br$$

- A **substitution reaction** occurs when an atom or group in one compound is replaced by an atom or group from another substance. For example:

  $$CH_3CH_2Cl + NaOH \longrightarrow CH_3CH_2OH + NaCl$$

- An **elimination reaction** occurs when the components of a simple molecule are removed from an organic molecule and are *not* replaced by other atoms or groups. For instance a hydrogen atom, H, and a hydroxy group, –OH, could be removed, forming water. This happens with ethanol in the presence of concentrated sulphuric acid.

  $$CH_3CH_2OH \longrightarrow H_2C=CH_2 + H_2O$$

- An **electrophile** is an atom, ion or group that, when forming a covalent bond, attacks an electron-rich site and accepts a pair of electrons from that site. Examples include HBr, Br_2, NO_2^+, CH_3^+ and CH_3C^+O.

- A **nucleophile** is an atom, ion or group that attacks a δ^+ atom and donates a lone pair of electrons to that atom, forming a covalent bond. Examples include H_2O, NH_3, OH^- and CN^-.

- A **free radical** is an atom or group with an unpaired electron. Examples include Cl• and CH_3•.

Aromatic compounds

Aromatic compounds contain a benzene ring.

Structure of benzene, C_6H_6

Benzene is a cyclic compound that has six carbon atoms in a hexagonal ring.

Early theories suggested that there were alternate single and double bonds between the carbon atoms, but this did not fit with later experimental evidence. It was shown that all the carbon–carbon bonds are the same length and that the molecule is planar.

Two modern theories are used to explain the structure.

- The Kekulé version assumes that benzene is a **resonance hybrid** between the two structures:

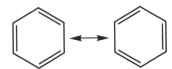

- The other theory assumes that each carbon atom is joined by a σ-bond to each of its two neighbours and by a third σ-bond to a hydrogen atom. The fourth bonding electron is in a *p*-orbital, and the six *p*-orbitals overlap above and below the plane of the ring of carbon atoms. This produces a **delocalised** π-system of electrons, as in:

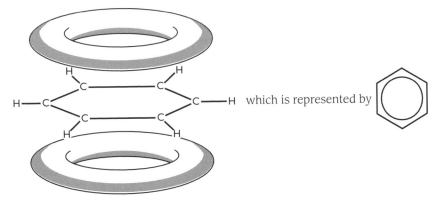

which is represented by

Thus, benzene, is more stable than 'cyclohexatriene', which is the theoretical compound with three single and three double carbon–carbon bonds. The amount by which it is stabilised can be calculated from the enthalpies of hydrogenation.

cyclohexene + $H_2(g) \longrightarrow$ cyclohexane $\Delta H = -119\,\text{kJ mol}^{-1}$

Therefore, ΔH for the addition to three localised double bonds in 'cyclohexatriene' would be $3 \times -119 = -357\,\text{kJ}$. However:

benzene + $3H_2(g) \longrightarrow$ cyclohexane $\Delta H = -207\,\text{kJ mol}^{-1}$

Thus, 150 kJ *less* energy is given out because of benzene's unique structure. This is called the **delocalisation stabilisation energy** or **resonance energy** and can be shown in an enthalpy level diagram.

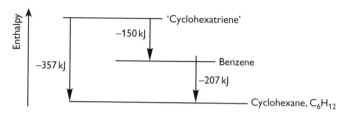

The amount by which it is stabilised can also be calculated from average bond enthalpies. The enthalpy of formation of gaseous is $+83\,kJ\,mol^{-1}$.

The value for the theoretical molecule 'cyclohexatriene' can be found using the Hess's law cycle below:

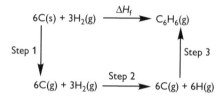

Step 1 equals 6 × enthalpy of atomisation of carbon (ΔH_a) = 6 × (+715) = +4290 kJ

Step 2 equals 3 × H–H bond enthalpy = 3 × (+436) = +1308 kJ

Step 3 — bonds made:
- three C–C = 3 × (–348) = –1044 kJ
- three C=C = 3 × (–612) = –1836 kJ
- six C–H = 6 × (–412) = –2472 kJ
- total = –5352 kJ

The ΔH_f of 'cyclohexatriene' = $\Delta H_{step\,1}$ + $\Delta H_{step\,2}$ + $\Delta H_{step\,3}$ = +4290 + 1308 + (–5352) = +246 kJ mol^{-1}. This is 163 kJ more than the experimental value of 'real' benzene, which is +83 kJ mol^{-1}. The difference is the value of the resonance energy and is not quite the same as that calculated by the first method because it has been calculated using *average* bond enthalpies.

Reactions of benzene

Benzene reacts by **electrophilic substitution**. A catalyst is *always* needed, since delocalisation causes the reactions to have large activation energies.

Reaction with bromine: halogenation

Dry benzene reacts with liquid bromine in the presence of a catalyst of iron (or anhydrous iron(III) bromide). Steamy fumes of hydrogen bromide are given off and bromobenzene, C_6H_5Br, is formed.

Reaction with nitric acid: nitration

When benzene is warmed with a mixture of concentrated nitric and sulphuric acids, a nitro- group, NO_2, replaces a hydrogen atom in the benzene ring. Nitrobenzene and water are produced.

The sulphuric acid reacts with the nitric acid to form the electrophile, NO_2^+. The temperature must not go above 50°C or some dinitrobenzene, $C_6H_4(NO_2)_2$, will be formed.

Friedel–Crafts reaction

Reaction with halogenoalkanes

In the presence of an anhydrous aluminium chloride catalyst, alkyl groups (e.g. C_2H_5) can be substituted into the ring. In the reaction between benzene and iodoethane, the products are ethylbenzene and hydrogen iodide.

The reaction mixture must be *dry*.

Reaction with acid chlorides

In the presence of an anhydrous aluminium chloride catalyst, benzene reacts with acid chlorides to form ketones. In the reaction between benzene and ethanoyl chloride, the products are phenylethanone and hydrogen chloride.

The reagents must be *dry*.

Reactions of aromatic compounds with a carbon-containing side chain

When a compound with a carbon atom attached to a benzene ring is heated under reflux with the oxidising agent potassium manganate(VII) dissolved in aqueous sodium hydroxide, each side chain, *whatever its type or length*, is converted to a COO^- group. The purple solution changes to a brown precipitate of manganese(IV) oxide. On acidification, a carboxylic acid (e.g. benzoic acid, C_6H_5COOH) is formed.

$$C_6H_5C_2H_5 + OH^- + 6[O] \longrightarrow C_6H_5COO^- + 3H_2O + CO_2$$

If two side chains are present, a dicarboxylate ion is formed.

$$CH_3C_6H_4COCH_3 + 2OH^- + 7[O] \longrightarrow {^-}OOCC_6H_4COO^- + 4H_2O + CO_2$$

Phenol

Phenol, C_6H_5OH, contains an –OH group on a benzene ring. A lone pair of electrons on the oxygen atom becomes part of the delocalised π-system and makes phenol more susceptible to attack by electrophiles. Also, the H atom in the –OH group becomes more δ^+, and so phenol is a weak acid — weaker than a carboxylic acid such as ethanoic, CH_3COOH, but stronger than water.

Reaction with bases

Phenol reacts with aqueous sodium hydroxide to form a solution of sodium phenate.

$$C_6H_5OH(aq) + NaOH(aq) \longrightarrow C_6H_5ONa(aq) + H_2O(l)$$

Phenol is not a strong enough acid to displace carbon dioxide from carbonates.

Reaction with bromine

The electron-rich ring in phenol is attacked by bromine water, in an electrophilic substitution reaction. The brown bromine water is decolourised and a white precipitate of 2,4,6-tribromophenol and a solution of hydrogen bromide are formed. No catalyst is needed.

Electrophilic substitution reactions are typical of aromatic compounds.

Reaction with acid chlorides

A *dry* mixture of phenol and ethanoyl chloride reacts to form the ester phenyl ethanoate and steamy fumes of gaseous hydrogen chloride.

$$C_6H_5OH + CH_3COCl \longrightarrow C_6H_5OOCCH_3 + HCl$$

In this reaction, phenol is acting as an alcohol. Unlike ethanol, it is not sufficiently alcoholic to form an ester with a carboxylic acid, such as ethanoic acid.

Phenylamine

Phenylamine is an aromatic amine with an –NH_2 group attached to the benzene ring.

Preparation

When nitrobenzene (made by the reaction of benzene with concentrated nitric and sulphuric acids) is heated under reflux with a mixture of tin and concentrated hydrochloric acid, it is reduced to an amine salt, which is then treated with sodium hydroxide solution to liberate phenylamine. The overall reaction is:

$$C_6H_5NO_2 + 6[H] \longrightarrow C_6H_5NH_2 + 2H_2O$$

Reaction as a base

Phenylamine is a weak base (weaker than ethylamine because the lone pair of electrons on the nitrogen atom is partially drawn into the ring), so it reacts with strong acids such as hydrochloric acid. The insoluble covalent liquid phenylamine forms a colourless solution of the ionic salt phenylammonium chloride.

$$C_6H_5NH_2(l) + HCl(aq) \longrightarrow C_6H_5NH_3^+Cl^-(aq)$$

Reaction with nitrous acid

Nitrous acid reacts with phenylamine in acid solution to form diazonium ions.

$$C_6H_5NH_2 + H^+ + HNO_2 \longrightarrow C_6H_5N_2^+ + 2H_2O$$

The nitrous acid has to be made in situ by adding cold sodium nitrite solution to cold dilute hydrochloric acid. The reaction mixture must be maintained above 0°C (otherwise the reaction is too slow) and below 10°C (or the diazonium ion decomposes).

Formation of azo dyes

Diazonium ions are not stable to heat but solutions can be reacted with phenol to form highly coloured, insoluble azo dyes. For example, if a benzenediazonium ion solution is added to phenol in sodium hydroxide solution, a yellow precipitate is obtained:

$$\bigcirc\!\!-\!\!\overset{+}{N}\!\!\equiv\!\!N \,+\, \bigcirc\!\!-\!\!OH + OH^- \longrightarrow \bigcirc\!\!-\!\!N\!\!=\!\!N\!\!-\!\!\bigcirc\!\!-\!\!OH + H_2O$$

Reaction mechanisms

How to write mechanisms

A **curly arrow** represents the movement of a pair of electrons:

The curly arrow must:

- start either from an atom (preferably drawn from a lone pair of electrons on that atom) or from a σ- or π-bond
- go towards an atom, where it will either form a bond or turn into a negative ion
- always be used in electrophilic and nucleophilic mechanisms

In the example below, the π-electrons move towards the H atom, forming a new C–H bond and the σ-electrons in the H–Br bond move to the Br atom, forming a Br⁻ ion.

In the next example, the lone pair of electrons moves towards the carbon atom, forming a new O–C bond. Simultaneously, the electrons in the C–Cl σ-bond move to the Cl atom, forming a Cl⁻ ion.

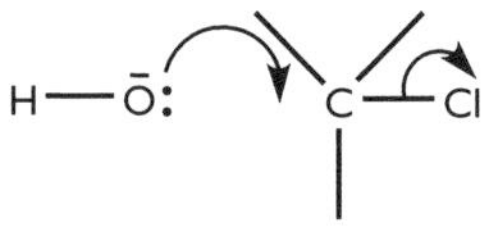

$$H—\ddot{O}: \quad C—Cl$$

A **half-headed arrow** represents the movement of a *single* electron from a bond to an atom, whereby a free radical is formed:

Half-headed arrows are only used in free-radical mechanisms. For example:

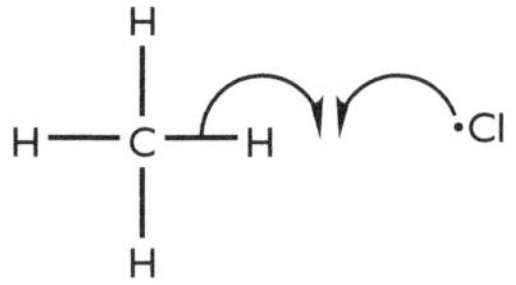

$$H—C—H \quad \cdot Cl$$

One of the electrons in the C–H σ-bond moves towards the chlorine radical and forms a new H–Cl σ-bond with the chlorine's unpaired electron.

Types of reaction mechanism
Free radical substitution in alkanes
An example is the reaction between a halogen (usually chlorine) and an alkane, such as methane. Visible or ultraviolet light is needed to initiate the reaction.

- **Initiation:** Cl_2 + light energy $\longrightarrow$ 2Cl•
- **Propagation:** the chlorine radical removes a hydrogen atom from a methane molecule, forming a hydrogen chloride molecule and a methyl radical.

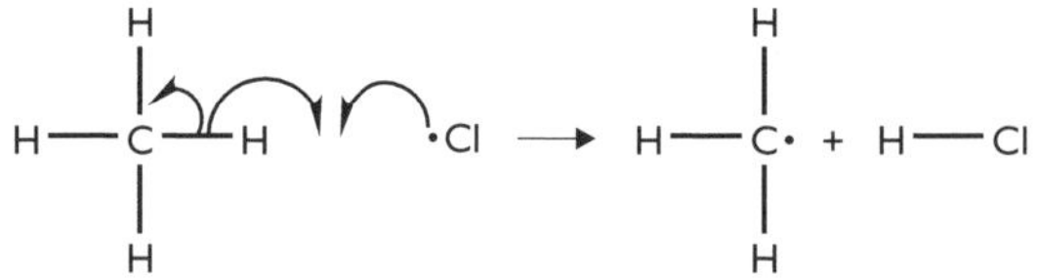

$$H—C—H \quad \cdot Cl \longrightarrow H—C\cdot + H—Cl$$

The methyl radical then removes a chlorine atom from a chlorine molecule, forming a chloromethane molecule and a chlorine radical, which then continues the process.

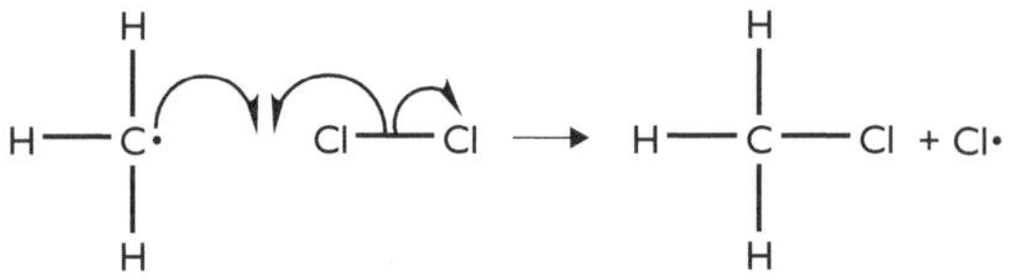

$$H—C\cdot \quad Cl—Cl \longrightarrow H—C—Cl + Cl\cdot$$

- **Termination:** if two radicals meet, the chain process is broken.

  $$CH_3\bullet + CH_3\bullet \longrightarrow C_2H_6$$

Free radical addition to alkenes

An example of this type of reaction is addition polymerisation of alkenes, such as ethene. An initiator is added that forms radicals (R•), which then attack the double bond and attach to one of the carbon atoms, with the other becoming a radical.

$$R\bullet + H_2C=CH_2 \longrightarrow RCH_2CH_2\bullet$$

This then adds on to another ethene molecule.

$$RCH_2CH_2\bullet + H_2C=CH_2 \longrightarrow RCH_2CH_2CH_2CH_2\bullet$$

This is repeated thousands of times.

Electrophilic addition to alkenes

This is the reaction of alkenes with electrophiles such as halogens and hydrogen halides.

Reaction with bromine

Step 1: As the bromine molecule approaches, the π-electrons move towards one bromine atom, causing the σ-electrons in the Br–Br bond to move to the other bromine atom. An intermediate carbonium ion is formed, together with a Br$^-$ ion.

Step 2: The Br$^-$ ion adds on from the opposite side, forming the product, 1,2-dibromoethane.

Reaction with hydrogen bromide

Step 1: This is similar to the reaction with bromine. A carbonium ion is formed by the addition of H$^+$.

Step 2: The halide ion adds on. If the alkene is unsymmetrical (e.g. propene), it is energetically favourable to form a *secondary* carbonium ion rather than a primary one in step 1.

Secondary carbonium ion

The major product is 2-bromopropane.

This can be *predicted* but not *explained* by Markovnikov's rule, which states that when a hydrogen halide adds to an unsymmetrical alkene, the hydrogen adds on to the carbon that already has more hydrogen atoms directly attached to it.

It should be noted that in both the above reactions, the electrophile (Br_2 or HBr) accepts a *pair* of electrons from the π-bond.

Electrophilic substitution in benzene

Benzene reacts with halogens, nitric acid, halogenoalkanes and acid chlorides by an electrophilic substitution mechanism. The mechanism is similar in all four reactions, but the formation of the electrophile differs. A catalyst is required.

Reaction with bromine

The catalyst, anhydrous iron(III) bromide, is made by the reaction of iron with bromine.

$$Fe + 1\tfrac{1}{2}Br_2 \longrightarrow FeBr_3$$

This then reacts with more bromine, forming the electrophile Br^+:

$$Br_2 + FeBr_3 \longrightarrow Br^+ + [FeBr_4]^-$$

Br^+ attacks the π-electrons in the benzene ring, forming an intermediate with a positive charge. Finally, the $[FeBr_4]^-$ ion removes an H^+ from benzene, producing hydrogen bromide, HBr, and re-forming the catalyst, $FeBr_3$.

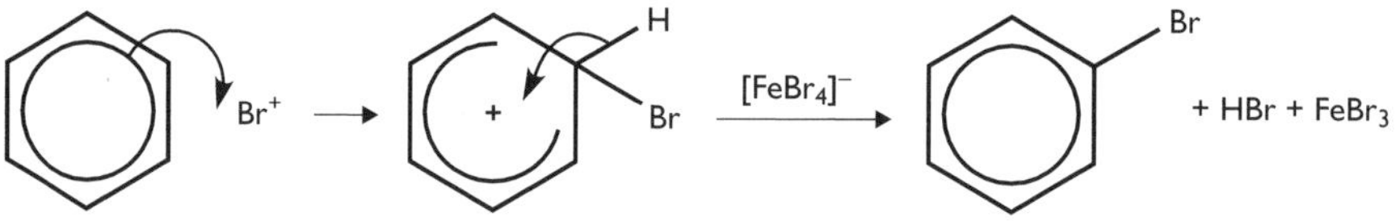

The addition of Br^+ to benzene is similar to the first step of the addition of bromine to ethene. The difference arises at the next step. The benzene intermediate loses an H^+, thus regaining the *stability of the delocalised* π-system, whereas the intermediate with ethene adds a Br^- ion. A catalyst must be present for the addition of Br^+ to benzene, because the activation energy is higher than that for the addition to ethene.

Reaction with nitric acid

Sulphuric acid protonates nitric acid because the sulphuric acid is a stronger acid.

$$H_2SO_4 + HNO_3 \longrightarrow H_2NO_3^+ + HSO_4^-$$

Acid 1   Base 2   Conjugate acid 2   Conjugate base 1

The $H_2NO_3^+$ ion loses a water molecule, forming the electrophile NO_2^+.

$$H_2NO_3^+ \longrightarrow H_2O + NO_2^+$$

NO_2^+ then attacks the benzene ring.

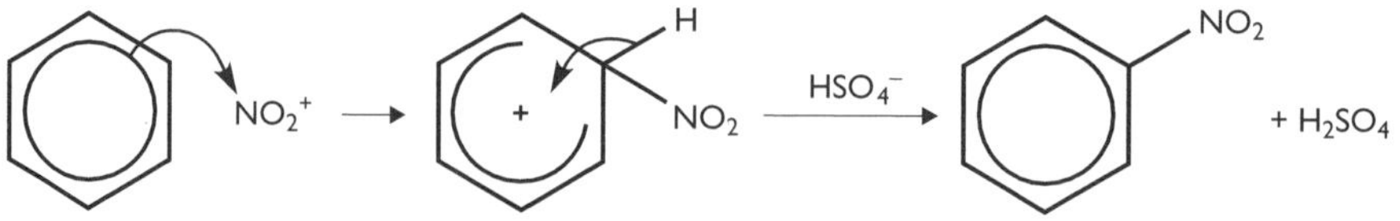

The H$^+$ combines with the HSO$_4^-$ ion produced in the protonation of the nitric acid, re-forming the catalyst, H$_2$SO$_4$.

Friedel–Crafts reaction with chloroethane and ethanoyl chloride
The anhydrous aluminium chloride catalyst removes the Cl$^-$ ion, forming [AlCl$_4$]$^-$ and an electrophile — CH$_3$CH$_2^+$ (from chloroethane) or CH$_3$C$^+$O (from ethanoyl chloride). The electrophile then reacts with benzene. For example:

The H$^+$ reacts with the [AlCl$_4$]$^-$ ion, producing hydrogen chloride and re-forming the catalyst, AlCl$_3$.

Tip The curly arrow from the delocalised π-ring must go to the correct carbon — not to the CH$_3$ carbon and not to the plus sign of CH$_3$C$^+$O.

Nucleophilic addition to aldehydes and ketones
An example is the reaction of carbonyl compounds with hydrogen cyanide.

Tip Note that the curly arrow goes from the C of the CN$^-$ ion and not from the nitrogen atom or from the minus sign of the CN$^-$ ion. These are common errors.

The conditions for the addition of hydrogen cyanide are critical, because CN$^-$ ions are needed for the first step and HCN molecules for the second. The usual method is to add sodium cyanide in a solution buffered at pH 5–8. The CN$^-$ ion is the nucleophile and uses the lone pair of electrons on the carbon atom to form a bond with the carbon atom of the carbonyl group. The negatively charged intermediate then removes an H$^+$ ion from an HCN molecule.

Nucleophilic substitution in halogenoalkanes
Reaction with hydroxide ions in aqueous sodium (or potassium) hydroxide
There are two different mechanisms, depending on the type of halogenoalkane. The first occurs with primary compounds such as 1-bromopropane.

As a pair of electrons moves from the oxygen to form a bond with the carbon atom, the σ-bond between the carbon and the bromine begins to break. The OH⁻ ion is the nucleophile as it uses a lone pair to form a bond with the carbon atom. This mechanism is called S_N2 (**nucleophilic substitution 2**), because two species are involved in the rate-determining step and the reaction is second-order (see p. 48). The rate of reaction is I > Br > Cl, because the C–I bond is the weakest and the C–Cl bond the strongest.

Note: if the halogenoalkane is optically active, the alcohol produced is also optically active.

The second type of mechanism occurs with tertiary compounds such as 2-bromo-2-methylpropane.

The first step is the formation of a carbonium ion. This is a relatively slow process and so is rate-determining. The carbonium ion then rapidly picks up an OH⁻ ion. As there is only one species on the left of the rate-determining step, the reaction is first-order and takes place by an S_N1 **mechanism**.

Note: if the halogenoalkane is optically active, the product alcohol is the racemic mixture. This is because the intermediate carbonium ion is planar with three pairs of electrons around the carbon atom, and the OH⁻ ion can attack from either the top or the bottom.

Secondary compounds react by both the mechanisms simultaneously. The rate of reaction is in the order tertiary > secondary > primary.

Note: if the halogenoalkane is reacted with a solution of potassium hydroxide in ethanol, an elimination reaction takes place instead of the substitution described above.

$$CH_3CHBrCH_3 + KOH \longrightarrow CH_3CH=CH_2 + KBr + H_2O$$

Reaction with cyanide ions in aqueous/ethanolic solutions of sodium cyanide
The mechanism is the same as with hydroxide ions. The lone pair of electrons on the carbon atom of the CN⁻ ion attacks the carbon atom in the halogenoalkane and at the same time the carbon–halogen bond breaks.

Note: hydrogen cyanide and sodium cyanide do *not* react with alcohols.

Synoptic questions on mechanisms
Parts of the Unit 5 test involve synoptic issues — this is especially likely in organic questions. One way that this can be achieved is to ask about related mechanisms. For instance, you could be asked to suggest the first steps in the reaction of ammonia with halogenoalkanes (nucleophilic substitution) or of lithium aluminium hydride with

compounds containing the C=O group (nucleophilic addition by the H^- ion). Remember that nucleophiles provide a lone pair of electrons to form a bond with a δ^+ site.

Another synoptic question could ask you to explain why the reactions of bromine with benzene and of bromine with ethene have different mechanisms.

Aromatic reactions summary

You should learn the following reactions.

Reactions of benzene

Reagent	Equation	Conditions	Products
With nitric acid	$C_6H_6 + HNO_3$ $\longrightarrow C_6H_5NO_2 + H_2O$	Concentrated nitric and sulphuric acids, 50°C	Nitrobenzene and water
With bromine	$C_6H_6 + Br_2$ $\longrightarrow C_6H_5Br + HBr$	Dry, with a catalyst of iron or anhydrous $FeBr_3$	Bromobenzene and hydrogen bromide
With chloromethane	$C_6H_6 + CH_3Cl$ $\longrightarrow C_6H_5CH_3 + HCl$	Dry, with anhydrous aluminium chloride catalyst	Methylbenzene and hydrogen chloride
With ethanoyl chloride	$C_6H_6 + CH_3COCl$ $\longrightarrow C_6H_5COCH_3 + HCl$	Dry, with anhydrous aluminium chloride catalyst	Phenylethanone and hydrogen chloride

Side-chain oxidation

All compounds with a carbon atom attached to a benzene ring can be oxidised to the salt of a carboxylic acid, with the COO^- group attached to the ring.

$$C_6H_5CH_2CH_2OH + 5[O] + NaOH \longrightarrow C_6H_5COONa + 3H_2O + CO_2$$

The mixture is heated under reflux with potassium manganate(VII) in aqueous sodium hydroxide. The products are sodium benzoate, water and carbon dioxide.

Reactions of phenol

Reagent	Equation	Products
With aqueous sodium hydroxide	$C_6H_5OH + NaOH \longrightarrow C_6H_5ONa + H_2O$	Sodium phenate and water
With bromine water	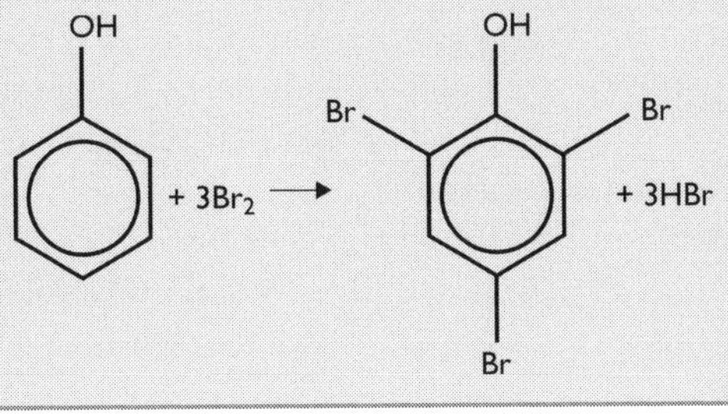	2,4,6-tribromophenol and hydrogen bromide

Reduction of nitrobenzene

Nitrobenzene is reduced by warming under reflux with tin and concentrated hydrochloric acid.

$$C_6H_5NO_2 + 6[H] \longrightarrow C_6H_5NH_2 + 2H_2O$$

The products are phenylamine and water.

Reactions of phenylamine

Reagent	Equation	Conditions	Products
With acid chloride	$C_6H_5NH_2 + HCl$ $\longrightarrow C_6H_5NH_3{}^+Cl^-$	n.a.	Phenylammonium chloride
With nitrous acid (made in situ from sodium nitrite and dilute hydrochloric acid)	$C_6H_5NH_2 + HNO_2$ $+ HCl \longrightarrow$ $C_6H_5N_2{}^+Cl^- + 2H_2O$	Aqueous solution between 0 and 10°C	Phenyldiazonium chloride and water

Reaction of diazonium ions with phenol

Diazonium ions react at 5°C with phenol in a solution of aqueous sodium hydroxide.

The product is a yellow precipitate of 4-hydroxyazobenzene.

Chemical kinetics

Required AS chemistry

You are expected to know the kinetics studied in Unit 2. In particular, you should have a thorough understanding of collision theory, including the Maxwell–Boltzmann distribution of molecular energies.

Collision theory

The following are important factors:

- **Collision frequency** — how often the molecules collide in a given time.
- **Collision energy** — particles must collide with enough kinetic energy to cause reaction. The minimum energy that two molecules must have on collision in order to react is called the **activation energy**, E_a.
- **Orientation** on collision — no reaction will occur if the OH⁻ ion collides with the CH_3 group in the nucleophilic substitution reaction between, for example, chloroethane and hydroxide ions. The collision must occur with the carbon carrying the chlorine.

Maxwell–Boltzmann distribution

The molecules in a gas and a solution have a wide range of kinetic energies. This is shown graphically in the Maxwell–Boltzmann distribution at two temperatures, T_{cold} and T_{hot}.

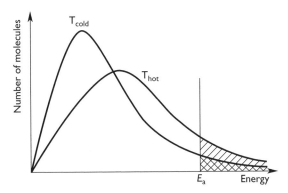

Note that both graphs start at the origin, but neither touches the x-axis at high energies. The difference between the two curves is that the curve for T_{hot}:

- has a lower modal value (the peak)
- has a modal value to the right of that of T_{cold}

Effect of temperature on rate

The *area* under the curve to the *right* of the activation energy (hatched on the above graphs) is a measure of the number of molecules that have enough energy to react on collision.

This area is greater on the T_{hot} graph compared with the T_{cold} graph. Therefore, the number of collisions between molecules with enough energy to react is greater. This means that a greater *proportion* of the collisions will result in reaction, so the rate of reaction will be faster at the higher temperature.

Effect of catalyst on rate

A catalyst causes the reaction to proceed by an *alternative route* that has a *lower* activation energy.

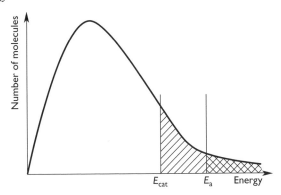

On the graph above, the value of E_{cat} is less than that of E_a, and so the area under the curve to the right of E_{cat} is greater than the area to the right of E_a. This means that a greater *proportion* of molecules will have the required lower activation energy on collision, allowing reaction to occur.

Effect of concentration and pressure on rate

An increase in the concentration of a reactant in solution, or in the pressure for gaseous reactions, increases the *frequency* of collisions. Therefore, the reaction rate increases.

Kinetic and thermodynamic stability

A mixture is kinetically stable if the activation energy is so high that the reaction is too slow to be observed at room temperature.

A reaction mixture is said to be thermodynamically stable *in relation* to the products if the enthalpy of the products is higher than that of the reactants. This means that the reaction would be endothermic.

A2 chemistry

Definitions

- The **rate of reaction** is the amount by which the concentration changes in a given time. Its units are $mol\,dm^{-3}\,s^{-1}$. To determine reaction rate, the concentration of a reactant or product is measured at regular time intervals and a graph of concentration against time is plotted.
  - The *slope (gradient)* of this line at a given point is the rate of reaction at that point.
  - The slope is calculated by dividing the *change* in concentration by the time difference (see pages 46–47).
  - The *initial* rate of reaction is calculated from the slope at time zero.
- The **rate equation** connects the rate of a reaction with the concentration of the reactants. For a reaction
    $$xA + yB \longrightarrow \text{products}$$
  the rate equation is
    $$\text{rate} = k[A]^m[B]^n$$
  where m and n may or may not be the same as x and y.

Note: if the reaction is carried out in the presence of a **homogeneous** catalyst, the concentration of the catalyst will appear in the rate equation. (Homogeneous means that all the reactants are in the same phase; either the gas phase or in solution.)

- The **order of reaction** is the sum of the powers to which the concentrations of the reactants are raised in the rate equation. In the example above, the order is $(m + n)$.
- The **partial order** with respect to one reactant is the power to which its

concentration is raised in the rate equation. In the example above, the partial order with respect to A is *m*.

- The **rate constant**, **k**, is the constant of proportionality that connects the rate of the reaction with the concentration of the reactants, as shown in the above rate equation. Its value alters with temperature. A reaction with a *large* activation energy has a *low* value of *k*.

Deducing the order of reaction

From initial rate data

To do this, you need data from at least three experiments. For example, data from the reaction below could be used:

$$xA + yB \longrightarrow \text{products}$$

Experiment	[A]/mol dm^{-3}	[B]/mol dm^{-3}	Initial rate/mol dm^{-3} s^{-1}
1	0.1	0.1	*p*
2	0.2	0.1	*q*
3	0.2	0.2	*r*

Comparing experiments 1 and 2 shows that [A] has doubled but [B] has stayed the same.

- If the rate is unaltered ($q = p$), the order with respect to A is 0.
- If the rate doubles ($q = 2p$), the order with respect to A is 1.
- If the rate quadruples ($q = 4p$), the order with respect to A is 2.

The order with respect to B can be determined in a similar way, by analysing experiments 2 and 3.

Worked example

In the table above, suppose $p = 0.0024$, $q = 0.0096$ and $r = 0.0096$.

- Determine the partial orders of A and B.
- Determine the total order.
- Write the rate equation.
- Calculate the value of the rate constant.

Answer

- From experiments 1 and 2: when [A] doubles, the rate quadruples ($0.0096 = 4 \times 0.0024$). Therefore, the order with respect to A is 2.
- From experiments 2 and 3: when [B] doubles, the rate is unaltered. Therefore, the order with respect to B is zero.
- The total order is $2 + 0 = 2$
- The rate equation is:

    rate = $k[A]^2$

- The rate constant is:

$$k = \frac{\text{rate}}{[A]^2} = \frac{0.0024 \text{ mol dm}^{-3} \text{ s}^{-1}}{(0.1 \text{ mol dm}^{-3})^2} = 0.24 \text{ mol}^{-1} \text{ dm}^3 \text{ s}^{-1}$$

From half-lives

The half-life is the time taken for the *concentration of a reactant to halve.* For a first-order reaction, the half-life is *constant.* Its value can be determined from a graph of concentration against time.

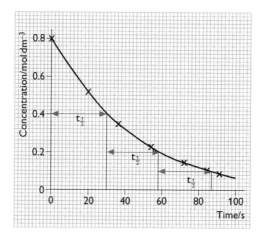

- The time taken for the concentration to halve from 0.8 to 0.4 mol dm^{-3} is 30 s.
- The time taken for the concentration to halve from 0.4 to 0.2 mol dm^{-3} is 28 s.
- The time taken for the concentration to halve from 0.2 to 0.1 mol dm^{-3} is 29 s.

The half-lives are *constant* to within experimental error and so the reaction is first-order. The average half-life is (30 + 28 + 29)/3 = 29 s.

From concentration–time data

- A graph is plotted with concentration on the *y*-axis and time on the *x*-axis.
- The initial rate of reaction is found by drawing a tangent to the curve at the starting concentration at time zero.
- The rate at another concentration (usually half the starting value) is found by drawing a tangent at that value.

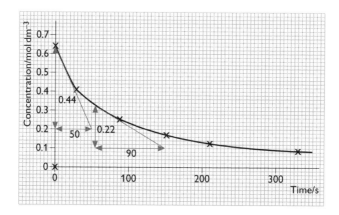

- The slope at the initial concentration is $(0.64 - 0.20)/50 = 0.0088 \, \text{mol dm}^{-3} \text{s}^{-1}$.
- The slope at $0.32 \, \text{mol dm}^{-3} = (0.32 - 0.10)/(150 - 60) = 0.0024 \, \text{mol dm}^{-3} \text{s}^{-1}$.

This value is close to $\frac{1}{4}$ that of the initial rate. As the rate decreased by a factor of 4 when the concentration halved, the reaction is second-order.

Note: for a second-order reaction, the value of the half-life *increases* as the concentration decreases. In the example above, the time taken for the concentration to fall from 0.64 to $0.32 \, \text{mol dm}^{-3}$ is 60 s; the time for the concentration to fall from 0.32 to $0.16 \, \text{mol dm}^{-3}$ is 120 s.

Rate constant

Calculation of the rate constant
You must first find the order of reaction.

From rate data
If you know the rate of reaction between substances A and B at given concentrations and the order of reaction with respect to A and B, the rate constant can be found using the equation:

$$k = \frac{\text{rate of reaction}}{[A]^m[B]^n}$$

where m and n are the known orders (see pages 44–45).

From the half-life
If you have plotted a graph of concentration against time and found that the half-life is constant, the reaction is first-order and the rate constant is given by the expression:

$$k = \frac{\ln 2}{t_{\frac{1}{2}}}$$

Rate constant units

Order	Units of k
Zero	$\text{mol dm}^{-3} \text{s}^{-1}$
First	s^{-1}
Second	$\text{mol}^{-1} \text{dm}^3 \text{s}^{-1}$

Effect of temperature on rate
An increase in temperature *always* increases the rate of a reaction. The mathematical relationship is given by the Arrhenius equation.

$$k = Ae^{-E_a/RT} \quad \text{or} \quad \ln k = \ln A - \frac{E_a}{RT}$$

where A is a constant, E_a is the activation energy, R is the gas constant and T is the temperature in K.

Tip You need not learn this equation. If it is needed, it will be given in the question.

The larger the value of T, the less negative is the power in the exponential term and so the larger the value of k. Using the logarithmic expression, the less negative the $-E_a/RT$ term, the larger $\ln k$ and k are. A *larger* value for k means a *faster* reaction.

A change in temperature does *not* alter the value of the activation energy. However, the Arrhenius equation also shows the relationship between activation energy and rate constant. A larger value of E_a gives a more negative exponential power and hence a smaller value of k. A *higher* activation energy results in a *slower* reaction.

A catalyst provides an alternative route with a lower activation energy. The *lower* E_{cat} results in a *larger* k and hence a *faster* reaction.

Reaction mechanisms

Partial orders and mechanisms

- Reactions often take place in two or more steps (see pages 37–40). The slowest step is called the **rate-determining step**.
- If the order with respect to a reactant is zero, then it must appear in the mechanism *after* the rate-determining step.
- If a reactant has a partial order of 2, then *two* molecules of it appear in the mechanism *up to and including* the rate-determining step.

The correctness of a mechanism can be tested by comparing it with the experimentally determined partial orders.

> **Worked example**
>
> The reaction
>
> $$2A + B \longrightarrow C + D$$
>
> was found to be first-order with respect to both A and B.
>
> Which of the following mechanisms is consistent with the data?
>
> *Mechanism I:*
>
> | | |
> |---|---|
> | **Step 1:** A + B $\longrightarrow$ intermediate | Fast |
> | **Step 2:** intermediate + A $\longrightarrow$ C + D | Slow |
>
> *Mechanism II:*
>
> | | |
> |---|---|
> | **Step 1:** B $\longrightarrow$ intermediate | Fast |
> | **Step 2:** intermediate + A $\longrightarrow$ C + X | Slow |
> | **Step 3:** X + A $\longrightarrow$ D | Fast |
>
> *Answer*
>
> In mechanism I, A appears twice and B once up to and including the rate-determining step. Therefore, the reaction would be second-order in A and first-order in B. This does not agree with the data.
>
> In mechanism II, A and B both appear only once up to and including the rate-determining step. Therefore, the reaction would be first order in both A and B, which is in agreement with the data.

Excess reactant

If one of the reactants is present in large excess, its concentration does not alter during the experiment, so it will *appear* to have a partial order of zero. The order of the reaction will depend only on the partial order of the other reactant. The hydrolysis of an ester in excess water is an example.

$$RCOOR' + H_2O \longrightarrow RCOOH + R'OH$$

If the concentration of the ester is monitored and plotted against time, the graph shows that the half-life is constant. This means that the reaction is first-order. As it is zero-order with respect to water, it is first-order with respect to the ester.

Intermediates and transition states

The S_N2 hydrolysis of a halogenoalkane occurs through a transition state, whereas the S_N1 reaction proceeds via an intermediate. The reaction profiles of these reactions are shown below:

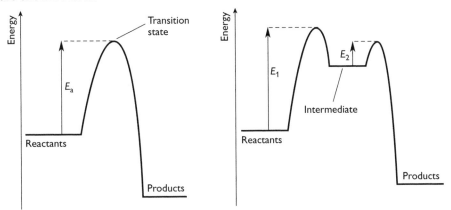

Note that as E_1 is greater than E_2, step 1 is rate-determining.

Methods of following a reaction

All the methods below must be carried out at *constant temperature*, preferably using a thermostatically controlled water bath.

Sampling

- Mix the reactants, stir and start timing.
- Remove samples at regular intervals and quench the reaction by adding the samples to iced water.
- Titrate samples against a suitable solution.

This method can be used when a reactant or product is:

- an acid — titrate against an alkali
- a base — titrate against an acid
- iodine — titrate against sodium thiosulphate solution, using starch as an indicator

Continuous monitoring

- If a gas is produced, *either* measure the volume of gas at regular intervals (collecting it over water in a measuring cylinder or using a gas syringe) *or* carry out the reaction on a top pan balance and measure the loss in mass at regular intervals.
- If a reactant or product is coloured, follow the reaction in a colorimeter. The intensity of the colour is a measure of the concentration.
- If a reactant is a single optical isomer, follow the reaction using a polarimeter. The angle of rotation depends on the concentration.

Note: Both a colorimeter and a polarimeter must first be *standardised* using a solution of known concentration. The use of a pH meter to follow the change in acidity is inaccurate.

The fixed point method

Some reactions can be followed by measuring the time taken to produce a fixed amount of a detectable product. The experiment is then repeated, changing the concentration of one of the reactants. In this type of experiment, the rate is calculated from the *reciprocal* of the time, i.e. 1/time measures the rate.

The reaction between dilute acid and aqueous sodium thiosulphate is an example. The reactants are mixed in a beaker standing on a tile marked with a large X. The time taken for enough sulphur to be precipitated to hide the X is measured.

Interpretation of graphical kinetic data

The most usual graphs have amount or concentration of reactant on the *y*-axis and time on the *x*-axis.

Example 1

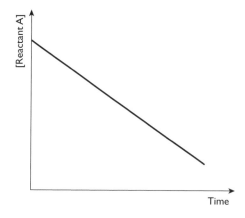

The slope is constant; therefore the rate is constant. The reaction is zero-order with respect to A.

content guidance

Example 2

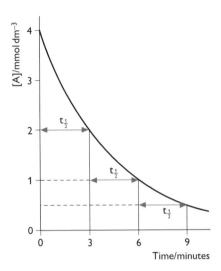

The half-life is constant, so the reaction is first-order with respect to A.

Example 3

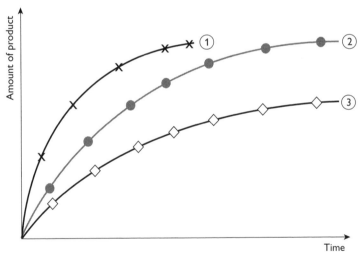

- Reaction 1 is the fastest — it has the steepest slope at the start.
- Reaction 2 is slower than 1 — it has a less steep slope at the start. The total amount of reactant is the same because both graphs level off at the same amount of product.
- Reaction 3 is the slowest — it has the least steep slope. Less reactant must have been present initially because the graph levels off at a lower amount of product.

Further organic chemistry

Required AS chemistry

Questions in Unit Test 5 require the application of knowledge of all the organic chemistry covered in this and previous units. Specific AS topics are nomenclature (you are expected to be able to name organic compounds), isomerism, reagents and reaction conditions. There is a list of all the organic reactions that you need to know at the end of this Content Guidance section.

Isomerism

Isomers have the same molecular formula but the atoms are arranged differently within the molecule.

Structural isomerism

- In **carbon chain** isomerism, the isomers have different carbon chain lengths. For instance, butane ($CH_3CH_2CH_2CH_3$) and methylpropane ($CH_3CH(CH_3)CH_3$) have the same molecular formula, C_4H_{10}.
- In **positional** isomerism, the same functional group is in one place in one isomer and in a different place in the other isomer — for example, propan-1-ol ($CH_3CH_2CH_2OH$) and propan-2-ol ($CH_3CH(OH)CH_3$).
- In **functional group** isomerism, the isomers are members of different homologous series. Examples are:
  - propanoic acid (CH_3CH_2COOH) and methylethanoate (CH_3COOCH_3)
  - ethanol (C_2H_5OH) and methoxymethane (CH_3OCH_3)
  - propanal (CH_3CH_2CHO) and propanone (CH_3COCH_3)

Tip If you are asked to draw a *full* structural formula, you must draw each bond and each atom separately.

Geometric isomerism

In an alkene, geometric (*cis–trans*) isomerism is the result of *restricted rotation* about a carbon–carbon double bond, provided that the two groups on each atom of the C=C group are different from each other.

The π-overlap in a double bond is above and below the line of the two carbon atoms. Therefore, it is not possible to rotate about the double bond without breaking the π-bond. This only happens at high temperatures and so the *cis* and *trans* isomers are different.

Optical isomerism

You should also revise optical isomerism from Unit 4.

A2 chemistry

Analysis

Chemical tests for functional groups

- You must give the *full* name or formula of the reagents used in any test.
- If a colour change is observed, you must state the colour *before* and *after* the test.

Alkenes

The functional group is C=C.

- Add bromine dissolved in water. The brown solution becomes colourless.
- Add *cold*, neutral potassium manganate(VII). The purple solution changes to a brown precipitate.

Halogenoalkanes

Warm with a little aqueous sodium hydroxide mixed with ethanol. Then acidify with dilute nitric acid and add silver nitrate solution.

The observation depends on the type of halogenoalkane:

- Chloroalkanes give a white precipitate soluble in dilute ammonia solution.
- Bromoalkanes give a cream precipitate insoluble in dilute ammonia solution but soluble in concentrated ammonia.
- Iodoalkanes give a yellow precipitate, insoluble in concentrated ammonia.

Hydroxyl groups in acids, alcohols and phenols

Add phosphorus pentachloride to the *dry* compound. Steamy fumes are given off.

Acids

Add aqueous sodium hydrogen carbonate. A gas is evolved that turns lime water cloudy.

Alcohols

To distinguish primary and secondary alcohols from tertiary alcohols, warm with potassium dichromate(VI) in dilute sulphuric acid:

- Primary and secondary alcohols turn the orange solution green.
- Tertiary alcohols do not react.

To distinguish between primary and secondary alcohols, test as above and distil the product into ammoniacal silver nitrate solution:

- Primary alcohols form a silver mirror.
- Secondary alcohols do not react.

Phenols

Add bromine water. The brown solution becomes colourless and a white precipitate forms.

Carbonyl compounds
Add 2,4-dinitrophenylhydrazine solution. A red-orange precipitate is produced.

To distinguish between aldehydes and ketones, add ammoniacal silver nitrate solution and warm:
- Aldehydes form a silver mirror.
- Ketones do not react.

Alternatively, add Fehling's solution and warm:
- Aldehydes produce a brown precipitate.
- Ketones do not react, so the blue solution remains.

Iodoform reaction
Add the test compound to a mixture of iodine and aqueous sodium hydroxide, or to a mixture of potassium iodide and sodium chlorate(I) solutions. A pale yellow precipitate is produced with the following:
- methyl ketones, because they contain the CH_3CO group
- ethanal, CH_3CHO
- secondary alcohols, because they contain the $CH_3CH(OH)$ group which is oxidised by the iodine to a methyl ketone

Spectroscopy
Mass spectra
In a mass spectrometer, molecules are bombarded with high-energy electrons. Positively charged ions are formed, which give rise to peaks in the mass spectrum. These peaks result from:
- the molecular ion, M^+, of mass/charge ratio (m/e) equal to the relative molecular mass of the substance. This is the ion with the *largest m/e* value in the spectrum.
- ionic fragments caused by the break-up of the molecular ion. The radicals lost provide information about the structure of the molecule under test.

m/e units lost	Group lost
15	CH_3
29	C_2H_5
31	CH_2OH

The mass spectrum of propan-1-ol is shown on page 57. The spectrum details are summarised in the following table.

Peak at m/e	Ionic fragment	Group lost
60	$(CH_3CH_2CH_2OH)^+$	None
45	$(CH_2CH_2OH)^+$	CH_3
31	$(CH_2OH)^+$	C_2H_5
29	CH_3CH_2	CH_2OH

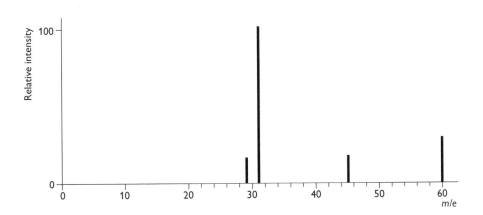

Propan-2-ol would give a peak at $m/e = 45$ due to loss of CH_3 but not at $m/e = 31$ because it does not have a C_2H_5 group.

Infrared spectra

An infrared spectrum is obtained by passing infrared radiation with a range of frequencies through a substance. The different bonds in the substance absorb radiation at a particular frequency, causing the bond to vibrate or twist. This results in a series of lines, each representing different bonds.

Broad bands are produced by O–H and N–H bonds, because of hydrogen bonding.

Approximate frequencies, measured in wave numbers, are shown in the following table.

Wave number/cm⁻¹	Group
1700	C=O
3300	O–H in alcohols
3000	O–H in acids
3400	N–H
2900	C–H

You will normally be given a table of frequencies and bonds. However, you ought to remember that:

- a sharp band around 1700 cm⁻¹ is caused by C=O in aldehydes, ketones, acids and esters
- a broad band around 3300 cm⁻¹ is caused by O–H in alcohols

The IR spectra below are of propan-1-ol and its oxidation product propanal. The propan-1-ol spectrum shows the broad alcohol O–H peak at 3300 cm⁻¹ and no peak around 1700 cm⁻¹. The propanal spectrum shows a sharp C=O peak at 1720 cm⁻¹ and no peak around 3300 cm⁻¹.

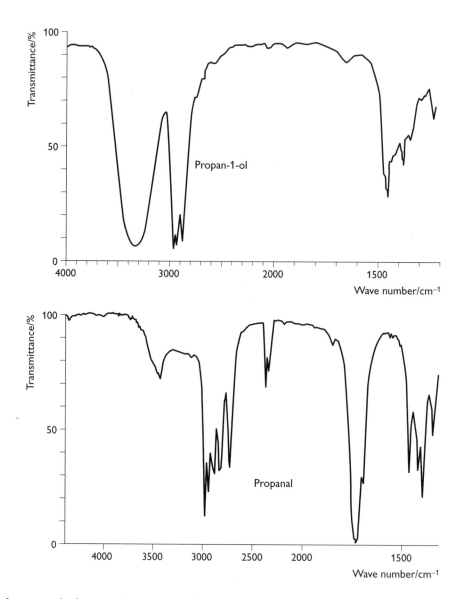

Propan-1-ol

Propanal

Low resolution nuclear magnetic resonance spectra

When placed in an extremely powerful external magnetic field, substances absorb radio frequency radiation. Spinning hydrogen nuclei produce a small magnetic field that can adopt a position parallel with, or at right angles to, the external magnetic field. As the hydrogen nuclei absorb radio-frequency energy, they flip between positions. The frequency of radio waves absorbed depends upon the chemical environment of the hydrogen atoms in the molecule. The amount that this differs from a reference substance is called the **chemical shift**, δ.

In propan-1-ol, $CH_3CH_2CH_2OH$, the hydrogen atoms are in four different environments. So, in the NMR spectrum, there are four peaks of intensity of absorption — 3:2:2:1 — because there are three hydrogen atoms in the CH_3 group, two in the next CH_2 group, two in the CH_2 group attached to the oxygen and one on the oxygen atom.

The NMR spectrum of propan-2-ol, $CH_3CH(OH)CH_3$, has three peaks — one of intensity 6 due to the six CH_3 hydrogens, one of intensity 1 due to the CH hydrogen and the third of intensity 1 due to the OH hydrogen. These are shown below, with the relative intensity written above each peak.

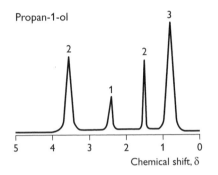 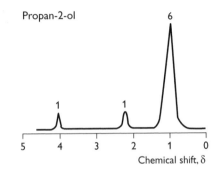

Ultraviolet and visible spectra

Compounds with C=C, C=O and N=N groups absorb radiation in the ultraviolet region. If the molecule has several alternate double and single bonds, the frequency of absorption shifts towards the visible region of the spectrum and the substance may be coloured. β-carotene contains a chain of 11 carbon–carbon double bonds alternating with single bonds. It absorbs visible light in the blue and green regions of the spectrum, and so the compound appears orange-red. β-carotene is present in carrots, which is why they are orange-red in colour.

Synthesis

You are expected to be able to deduce methods of converting one organic substance into another. Such methods often involve three or more steps. Sometimes the conversion may require the carbon chain length to be altered and this can be an important clue to the route.

Common reactions are listed below. Those marked * cause the carbon chain to be lengthened; those marked # cause the carbon chain to be shortened.
- *Primary alcohol* to an *aldehyde* (partial oxidation) — heat with potassium dichromate(VI) in dilute sulphuric acid and distil off the aldehyde as it forms.
- *Primary alcohol* to a *carboxylic acid* (complete oxidation) — heat under reflux with potassium dichromate(VI) in dilute sulphuric acid.
- *Secondary alcohol* to a *ketone* (oxidation) — heat under reflux with potassium dichromate(VI) in dilute sulphuric acid.

- *Alcohol* to a *halogenoalkane* — for example, add phosphorus pentachloride.
- *Halogenoalkane to a *Grignard* reagent — reflux with magnesium in dry ether. Then, react the Grignard reagent with:
  - carbon dioxide to produce a *carboxylic acid*
  - methanal to give a *primary alcohol*
  - an aldehyde to give a *secondary alcohol*
  - a ketone to give a *tertiary alcohol*
- *Halogenoalkane to a *nitrile* — add potassium cyanide in aqueous ethanol. (Alcohols do not react with potassium cyanide.)
- *Aldehyde or *ketone* to a *hydroxynitrile* — add hydrogen cyanide by reacting the carbonyl compound with potassium cyanide buffered at pH 6.
- *Nitrile* (or a hydroxynitrile) to a *carboxylic acid* (hydrolysis) — heat under reflux with dilute sulphuric acid.
- *Nitrile* to a *primary amine* (reduction) — lithium aluminum hydride in dry ether.
- *Benzene to an *alkyl benzene* or a *ketone* (Friedel–Crafts reaction) — with a halogenoalkane or an acyl chloride and an anhydrous aluminium chloride catalyst.
- # *Amides* to *amines* (Hofmann degradation) — heat under reflux with liquid bromine and then concentrated sodium hydroxide.
- # *Methyl ketone* (e.g. $RCOCH_3$) to a *carboxylic acid* (e.g. RCOOH) (iodoform reaction) — add iodine mixed with aqueous sodium hydroxide.

Practical techniques
You should be able to draw the sets of apparatus shown below.

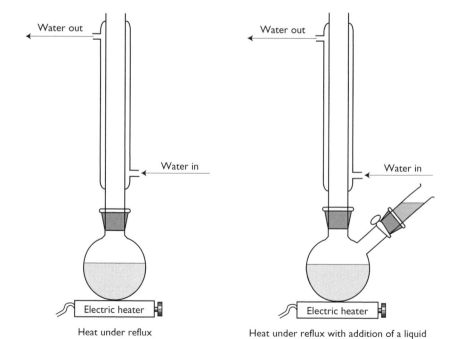

Heat under reflux   Heat under reflux with addition of a liquid

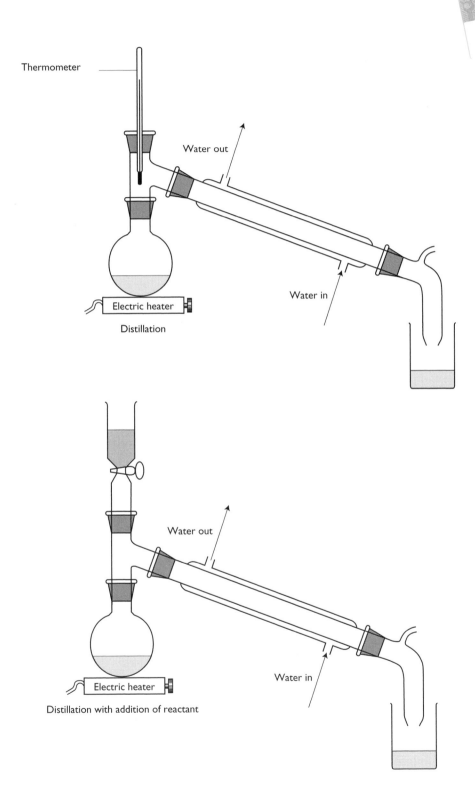

Distillation

Distillation with addition of reactant

- It is always safer to draw an electric heater rather than a bunsen burner, as a reactant or product might be flammable.
- Make sure that each piece of the apparatus is drawn as a separate piece and not fused to the next one. The joints between the different parts are difficult to draw.
- You must be able to draw a round-bottomed flask, a condenser (either in the reflux or distillation position) and a thermometer.
- Make sure that the water goes *in* at the *bottom* of the condenser and *out* at the *top*.
- Make sure that the apparatus is open to the air at some point — at the top of a reflux condenser or into a collecting vessel for distillation.

Heating under reflux
Heating under reflux is used when the reaction is slow and one of the reactants is volatile.

Fractional distillation
Fractional distillation is used to separate a mixture of two volatile liquids. When a liquid of composition x is heated in a fractional distillation apparatus, it will boil at a temperature T_1 (see diagram below).

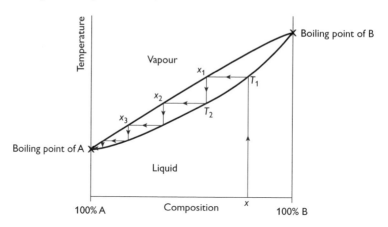

The vapour produced is richer in the more volatile substance, A, and has a composition x_1. This is condensed to a liquid by the cooler surface of the fractionating column, and begins to fall down the column where it is reboiled by the hot vapour rising up the column. The liquid boils at a temperature T_2, producing vapour of composition x_2 which is even richer in A.

This process is repeated and the composition of the vapour follows the line x_1, x_2, x_3 until eventually pure A is distilled off from the top of the column.

The liquid gets gradually richer in the less volatile substance B, and when all the A has been distilled off, pure B is left in the flask and can itself be distilled off.

Recrystallisation

Recrystallisation is used to purify a solid from other solid impurities:
- Dissolve the solid in the minimum amount of hot solvent.
- Filter the solution through a pre-heated glass filter funnel fitted with a fluted filter paper.
- Allow the filtrate to cool and crystals of the pure solid to appear.
- Filter using a Buchner funnel under reduced pressure. Wash the solid with a little cold solvent and allow to dry.

Melting and boiling point determinations

Melting and boiling point determinations are used as tests for the identity and purity of a substance.

Melting point

Heat the solid in a test tube immersed in a water-bath until it begins to melt. Measure the temperature. When the substance has completely melted, allow it to cool and measure the temperature at which it solidifies. The substance must be stirred all the time. Average the two temperatures.

Boiling point

Place the liquid in a test tube containing a thermometer with a capillary tube attached to it. The capillary tube is sealed at the upper end and the lower end is below the liquid surface.

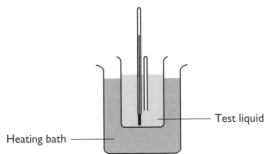

Heat the liquid in an oil- or water-bath with constant stirring. Measure the temperature when the liquid boils. Then allow it to cool and measure the temperature at the point when liquid is drawn up into the capillary tube. Average the two temperatures.

Special safety precautions for chemical reactions

- Carry out the reaction in a fume cupboard if a reactant or product is poisonous or is a harmful gas.
- Wear disposable gloves if a reactant or product is corrosive or is absorbed through the skin.
- Heat using a water-bath or an electric heater if a reactant or product is flammable. This is essential if ether is present in the reaction mixture.

Applied organic chemistry

Pharmaceuticals

Some pharmaceuticals must be water-soluble so that they can be transported in the bloodstream. Therefore, they must either be ionic or contain a high proportion of groups that can hydrogen bond to water. Aspirin contains a carboxylic acid group and converting it to its ionic sodium salt increases its solubility. Adrenaline, used to stimulate the heart in emergencies, contains three –OH groups and one –NH group, so it can form several hydrogen bonds with water and is soluble.

Other drugs need to be soluble in lipids. The neutral molecule *cis*-platin, $[Pt(NH_3)_2Cl_2]$, is lipid-soluble. It is used in the chemotherapeutic treatment of cancer.

Nitrogenous fertilisers

All plants need nitrogen to grow, but they cannot obtain it from the air. Ammonium salts, nitrates and urea are all fertilisers manufactured from ammonia. The cheapest is urea, which contains the highest proportion of available nitrogen. Urea releases nitrogen slowly and does not affect the pH of the soil. However, it is not suitable for all types of soil and cannot easily be made into pellets.

Natural fertilisers, such as compost, animal dung and slurry, are low in nitrogen. However, they help increase the humus in the soil, which makes the soil more water-retentive and fertile. Bacteria break down the organic compounds in natural fertilisers into inorganic chemicals, which plants can absorb.

Esters, fats and oils

Some esters are used as flavourings, perfumes and solvents for glue.

Animal fats are esters of *saturated* carboxylic acids (e.g. stearic acid, $C_{17}H_{35}COOH$) and propan-1,2,3-triol, $CH_2OHCH(OH)CH_2OH$. If animal fat is boiled with aqueous sodium hydroxide, sodium stearate ($C_{17}H_{35}COONa$) is formed. This is a soap and so the alkaline hydrolysis of an ester is called **saponification**.

Most vegetable oils are esters of *polyunsaturated* carboxylic acids and propan-1,2,3-triol. Vegetable oils can be hardened by reacting them with hydrogen in the presence of a nickel catalyst. The hydrogen adds to some of the double bonds. The product is margarine.

Polymers

Addition polymers

Addition polymers are formed when compounds containing a C=C group undergo polymerisation. Examples include:
- ethene to poly(ethene)
- propene to poly(propene)
- chloroethene to poly(chloroethene), which is called PVC
- tetrafluoroethene to poly(tetrafluoroethene) or PTFE
- phenylethene to poly(phenylethene) or polystyrene

The structures of some of these polymers are shown below:

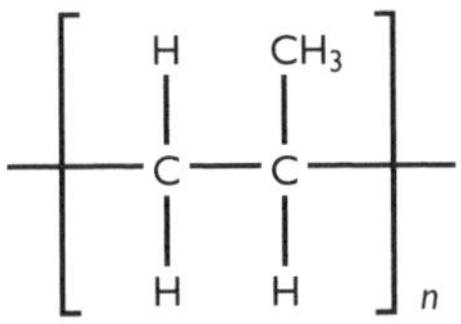

Poly(propene) 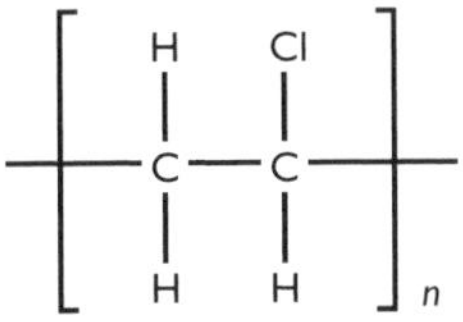   PVC 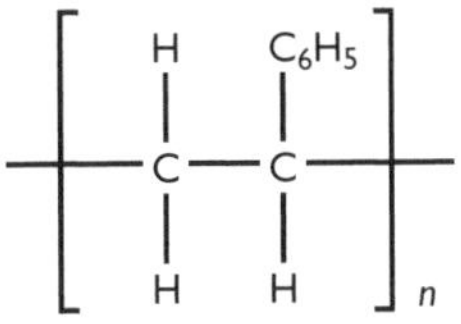   Polystyrene

Condensation polymers

Condensation polymers are formed when two compounds, each with two functional groups, polymerise. Water, or another simple molecule, is eliminated every time two molecules combine.

One example is the **polyester** terylene. A diol (e.g. ethan-1,2-diol, $HOCH_2CH_2OH$) reacts with a diacid (e.g. terephthalic acid, $HOOCC_6H_4COOH$), eliminating water and forming the polyester.

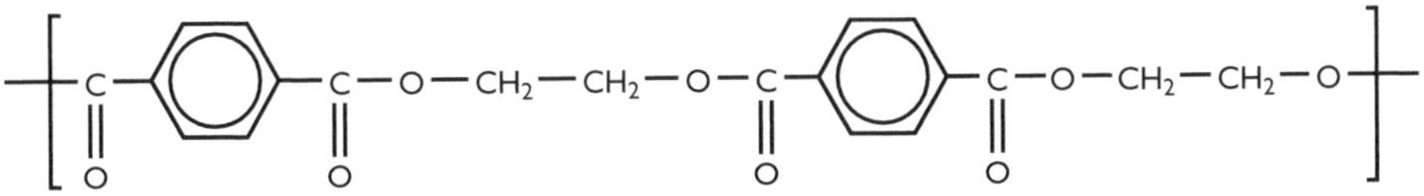

A polyester

Polyamides are also important condensation polymers. Nylon is an example. A diamine (e.g. 1,6-diaminohexane, $H_2N(CH_2)_6NH_2$) reacts with a diacid chloride (e.g. hexane-1,6-dioyl chloride, $ClOC(CH_2)_4COCl$), eliminating HCl and forming the polyamides.

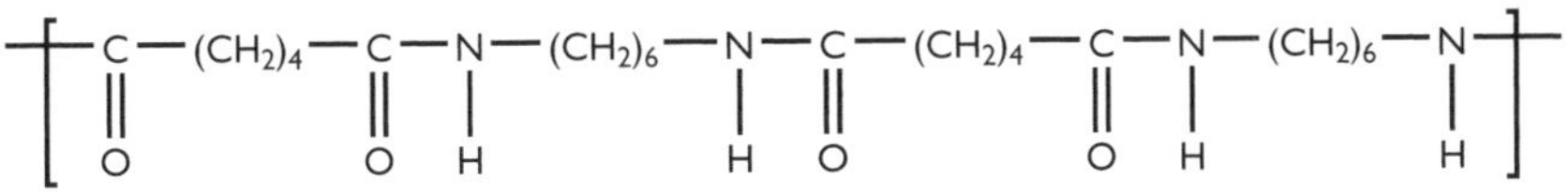

A polyamide

Environmental problems

Disposal is a problem with most polymers. They can cause litter and fill up landfill sites because they are stable and are not broken down by bacteria. However, their stability can be an advantage — for instance, the use of PVC for window frames.

If polymers are incinerated, they may produce poisonous fumes. Any chloro- polymer will produce harmful smoke containing hydrochloric acid and many will produce dioxins.

Organic reactions summary

Aromatic chemistry

These reactions are listed on pages 42–43.

Aliphatic chemistry
Alkanes

Reagent	Equation	Conditions	Products
Halogens (e.g. chlorine)	$CH_4 + Cl_2 \longrightarrow$ $CH_3Cl + HCl$	Light (visible or UV)	Chloromethane and hydrogen chloride
Oxygen (combustion)	$2C_2H_6 + 7O_2 \longrightarrow$ $4CO_2 + 6H_2O$	Burn or spark	Carbon dioxide and water

Alkenes

In the table below, propene is used as the example.

Reagent	Equation	Conditions	Products
Hydrogen	$CH_3CH=CH_2 + H_2$ $\longrightarrow CH_3CH_2CH_3$	Heated nickel catalyst	Propane
Halogens (e.g. bromine)	$CH_3CH=CH_2 + Br_2$ $\longrightarrow CH_3CHBrCH_2Br$	Bubble propene into bromine dissolved in hexane	1,2-dibromopropane
Hydrogen halides (e.g. hydrogen bromide)	$CH_3CH=CH_2 + HBr$ $\longrightarrow CH_3CHBrCH_3$	Mix gases at room temperature	2-bromopropane
Potassium manganate(VII) (oxidation)	$CH_3CH=CH_2 + [O]$ $+ H_2O \longrightarrow$ $CH_3CH(OH)CH_2OH$	Solution made alkaline with aqueous sodium hydroxide	Propan-1,2-diol

Alkenes polymerise. For example, at 2000 atm and 250°C propene polymerises to poly(propene):

$$nCH_3CH=CH_2 \longrightarrow (CH(CH_3)–CH_2)_n$$

Halogenoalkanes

In the table below, 2-iodopropane is used as the example.

Reagent	Equation	Conditions	Products
Aqueous sodium hydroxide	$CH_3CHICH_3 + NaOH$ $\longrightarrow CH_3CH(OH)CH_3$ $+ NaI$	Heat under reflux in *aqueous* solution	Propan-2-ol and sodium iodide
Ethanolic potassium hydroxide	$CH_3CHICH_3 + KOH$ $\longrightarrow CH_3CH=CH_2$ $+ KI + H_2O$	Heat under reflux in *ethanolic* solution	Propene, potassium iodide and water
Potassium cyanide	$CH_3CHICH_3 + KCN$ $\longrightarrow CH_3CH(CN)CH_3$ $+ KI$	Heat under reflux in a solution of water and ethanol	Methylpropanenitrile and potassium iodide
Ammonia	$CH_3CHICH_3 + 2NH_3$ $\longrightarrow CH_3CH(NH_2)CH_3$ $+ NH_4I$	Heat an ethanolic solution of ammonia in a sealed tube	2-aminopropane and ammonium iodide
Magnesium	$CH_3CHICH_3 + Mg$ $\longrightarrow CH_3CH(MgI)CH_3$	Reflux in dry ether solution	2-propylmagnesium iodide

Grignard reagents

In the table below, ethylmagnesium bromide is used as the example.

Reagent	Equation	Conditions	Organic product
Carbon dioxide	$C_2H_5MgBr + CO_2$ $\longrightarrow C_2H_5COOH$	Dry, solid carbon dioxide, followed by dilute hydrochloric acid	Propanoic acid
Methanal	$C_2H_5MgBr + HCHO$ $\longrightarrow C_2H_5CH_2OH$	Mix dry reagents, then add dilute hydrochloric acid	Propan-1-ol, a *primary* alcohol
Aldehydes (e.g. ethanal)	$C_2H_5MgBr + CH_3CHO$ $\longrightarrow C_2H_5CH(OH)CH_3$	Mix dry reagents, then add dilute hydrochloric acid	Butan-2-ol, a *secondary* alcohol
Ketones (e.g. propanone)	$C_2H_5MgBr +$ $CH_3COCH_3 \longrightarrow$ $C_2H_5C(OH)(CH_3)_2$	Mix dry reagents, then add dilute hydrochloric acid	2-methylbutan-2-ol, a *tertiary* alcohol

Alcohols

Oxidation

Primary alcohols (e.g. propan-1-ol) are oxidised by heating under reflux with sulphuric acid and potassium dichromate(VI).

$$C_2H_5CH_2OH + 2[O] \longrightarrow C_2H_5COOH + H_2O$$

The products are propanoic acid and water. However, if the oxidising agent is added to the hot alcohol and the product is distilled off as it is formed, propanal (C_2H_5CHO) is produced.

Secondary alcohols (e.g. propan-2-ol) can be oxidised in the same way. The product is a ketone (e.g. propanone).

Tertiary alcohols (e.g. 2-methylpropan-2-ol) cannot be oxidised.

Other reactions

Other reactions of primary alcohols are summarised in the table below, using propan-1-ol as the example.

Reagent	Equation	Conditions	Products
Concentrated sulphuric acid (dehydration)	$C_2H_5CH_2OH - H_2O$ $\longrightarrow CH_3CH=CH_2$	Heat to 170°C	Propene
Phosphorus pentachloride	$C_2H_5CH_2OH + PCl_5$ $\longrightarrow C_2H_5CH_2Cl + HCl$ $+ POCl_3$	Dry reagents at room temperature	1-chloropropane, hydrogen chloride and phosphorus oxychloride
Ethanoic acid	$C_2H_5CH_2OH +$ $CH_3COOH \longrightarrow$ $CH_3COOCH_2C_2H_5 + H_2O$	Warm gently with a few drops of concentrated sulphuric acid	1-propylethanoate and water

Reagent	Equation	Conditions	Products
Ethanoyl chloride	$C_2H_5CH_2OH +$ $CH_3COCl \longrightarrow$ $CH_3COOCH_2C_2H_5$ $+ HCl$	Mix dry reagents at room temperature	1-propylethanoate and hydrogen chloride
Hydrogen halide (e.g. HBr or HI)	$C_2H_5CH_2OH + HBr$ $\longrightarrow C_2H_5CH_2Br + H_2O$	HBr is made from 50% sulphuric acid and potassium bromide	1-bromopropane and water
	$C_2H_5CH_2OH + HI \longrightarrow$ $C_2H_5CH_2I + H_2O$	HI is made from damp red phosphorus and iodine	1-iodopropane and water

Carboxylic acids

In the table below, ethanoic acid is used as the example.

Reagent	Equation	Conditions	Products
Alkalis (e.g. sodium hydroxide)	$CH_3COOH + NaOH$ $\longrightarrow CH_3COO^-Na^+$ $+ H_2O$	Mix aqueous solutions	Sodium ethanoate and water
Alcohols (e.g. ethanol)	$CH_3COOH + C_2H_5OH$ $\longrightarrow CH_3COOC_2H_5$ $+ H_2O$	Warm with a few drops of concentrated sulphuric acid	Ethyl ethanoate and water
Phosphorus pentachloride	$CH_3COOH + PCl_5 \longrightarrow$ $CH_3COCl + HCl + POCl_3$	Mix dry reagents at room temperature	Ethanoyl chloride, hydrogen chloride and phosphorus oxychloride
Lithium aluminium hydride (reduction)	$CH_3COOH + 4[H] \longrightarrow$ $CH_3CH_2OH + H_2O$	Dry ether solution, then add dilute hydrochloric acid	Ethanol and water

Acid chlorides

In the table below, ethanoyl chloride is used as the example.

Reagent	Equation	Conditions	Products
Water	$CH_3COCl + H_2O \longrightarrow$ $CH_3COOH + HCl$	Room temperature	Ethanoic acid and hydrogen chloride
Alcohols (e.g. ethanol)	$CH_3COCl + C_2H_5OH \longrightarrow$ $CH_3COOC_2H_5 + HCl$	Dry reagents	Ethyl ethanoate and hydrogen chloride
Ammonia	$CH_3COCl + 2NH_3 \longrightarrow$ $CH_3CONH_2 + NH_4Cl$	Concentrated ammonia	Ethanamide and ammonium chloride
Amines (e.g. ethylamine)	$CH_3COCl + C_2H_5NH_2 \longrightarrow$ $CH_3CONHC_2H_5 + HCl$	Room temperature	A substituted amide and hydrogen chloride

Esters

In the table below, ethyl ethanoate is used as the example.

Reagent	Equation	Conditions	Products
Sodium hydroxide	$CH_3COOC_2H_5 + NaOH \longrightarrow CH_3COO^-Na^+ + C_2H_5OH$	Heat under reflux in aqueous solution	Sodium ethanoate and ethanol
Acids (e.g. sulphuric acid)	$CH_3COOC_2H_5 + H_2O \rightleftharpoons CH_3COOH + C_2H_5OH$	Heat under reflux with dilute sulphuric acid catalyst	Ethanoic acid and ethanol

Note: the reaction between ethyl ethanoate and sulphuric acid is reversible, so the yield of product is small.

Carbonyl compounds

Aldehydes and ketones

Ethanal is used as an example of an aldehyde and propanone as an example of a ketone.

- Reaction with 2,4-dinitrophenylhydrazine:

    $CH_3CHO + H_2NNHC_6H_3(NO_2)_2 \longrightarrow CH_3CH=NNHC_6H_3(NO_2)_2 + H_2O$
    $(CH_3)_2C=O + H_2NNHC_6H_3(NO_2)_2 \longrightarrow (CH_3)_2C=NNHC_6H_3(NO_2)_2 + H_2O$

    The product is an orange precipitate.

- Reaction with hydrogen cyanide:

    $CH_3CHO + HCN \longrightarrow CH_3CH(OH)CN$
    $CH_3COCH_3 + HCN \longrightarrow CH_3C(OH)(CN)CH_3$

    There must be some base present. The product is either 2-hydroxypropanenitrile (from ethanal) or 2-hydroxy-2-methylpropanenitrile (from propanone).

- Reduction with lithium aluminium hydride:

    $CH_3CHO + 2[H] \longrightarrow CH_3CH_2OH$
    $CH_3COCH_3 + 2[H] \longrightarrow CH_3CH(OH)CH_3$

    The reaction is carried out in a dry ether solution. The product is either ethanol (from ethanal) or propan-2-ol (from propanone).

Aldehydes

Aldehydes (e.g. ethanal) can be oxidised by warming gently with either ammoniacal silver nitrate or Fehling's solution.

$CH_3CHO + [O] + OH^- \longrightarrow CH_3COO^- + H_2O$

Ethanoate ions are produced. Ammoniacal silver nitrate gives a silver mirror; a red precipitate of copper(I) oxide forms with Fehling's solution.

Carbonyl compounds containing the CH_3CO group

If ethanal or methylketones are allowed to stand with iodine and sodium hydroxide, the following reaction occurs:

$RCOCH_3 + 3I_2 + 4NaOH \longrightarrow CHI_3 + 3NaI + RCOONa + 3H_2O$

The products are a yellow precipitate of iodoform (CHI_3) and the sodium salt of a carboxylic acid that has one carbon atom less than the original carbonyl compound.

Amines

In the table below, ethylamine is used as the example.

Reagent	Equation	Conditions	Products
Acids (e.g. hydrochloric)	$C_2H_5NH_2 + HCl \longrightarrow$ $C_2H_5NH_3{}^+Cl^-$	Mix aqueous solutions	Ethyl ammonium chloride
Acid chlorides (e.g. ethanoyl chloride)	$C_2H_5NH_2 + CH_3COCl \longrightarrow$ $CH_3CONHC_2H_5 + HCl$	Mix at room temperature	A substituted amide and hydrogen chloride

Amides

In the table below, ethanamide is used as the example. The reaction of amides with bromine and sodium hydroxide is called the Hofmann degradation reaction.

Reagent	Equation	Conditions	Products
Bromine and sodium hydroxide	$CH_3CONH_2 + Br_2 + 2NaOH$ $\longrightarrow CH_3NH_2 + 2NaBr$ $+ H_2O + CO_2$	Add liquid bromine and then heat with concentrated aqueous sodium hydroxide	Methylamine, sodium bromide, water and carbon dioxide
Phosphorus pentoxide	$CH_3CONH_2 - H_2O \longrightarrow$ CH_3CN	Heat	Ethanenitrile

Nitriles

In the table below, ethanenitrile is used as the example.

Reagent	Equation	Conditions	Products
Dilute hydrochloric acid (hydrolysis)	$CH_3CN + 2H_2O + HCl$ $\longrightarrow CH_3COOH + NH_4Cl$	Heat under reflux	Ethanoic acid and ammonium chloride
Lithium aluminium hydride (reduction)	$CH_3CN + 4[H] \longrightarrow$ $C_2H_5NH_2$	Dry ether solution	Ethylamine

Questions
&
Answers

The following questions are drawn from two recent A2 unit tests. Do not treat the answers as model answers or as rubber-stamp responses to be reproduced without thought. The most important reason for studying chemistry is to *understand* it, not merely to repeat it parrot-fashion — you have to do more than simply aim for a good grade.

In some instances, the difference between an A-grade response and a C-grade response has been suggested. This is not always possible, since many of the questions are rather short and do not require extended writing.

I do not suggest that this section covers all the possible questions that could be asked on Unit Test 5 — examiners are more resourceful than that. However, there are examples of questions on each topic of Unit 5.

Examiner's comments

Candidate responses to long-answer questions are followed by examiner's comments, preceded by the icon *e*. They are interspersed in the answers and indicate where credit is due. They also point out common errors that lower-grade answers are prone to show.

Unit Test 5, January 2003

Question 1

(a) The electronic structure of the cobalt atom can be written as $[Ar]3d^7 4s^2$.
Give the electronic structure of the Co^{3+} ion. (1 mark)

(b) (i) By reference to the standard electrode potentials given below, suggest
a reducing agent that might reduce aqueous Co^{3+} ions to cobalt
metal. Give your reasoning.

Half-equation	$E^{\ominus}/V$
$Zn^{2+}(aq) + 2e^- \rightleftharpoons Zn(s)$	−0.76
$Fe^{2+}(aq) + 2e^- \rightleftharpoons Fe(s)$	−0.44
$Co^{2+}(aq) + 2e^- \rightleftharpoons Co(s)$	−0.28
$Sn^{2+}(aq) + 2e^- \rightleftharpoons Sn(s)$	−0.14
$O_2(g) + 2H^+(aq) + 2e^- \rightleftharpoons H_2O_2(aq)$	+0.68
$Co^{3+}(aq) + e^- \rightleftharpoons Co^{2+}(aq)$	+1.82

(3 marks)

   (ii) Suggest two factors that might prevent a reducing agent from being
as effective as the electrode potentials might seem to suggest. (2 marks)

(c) (i) Write the formula of the hexaaquacobalt(II) ion. (1 mark)

   (ii) Give an equation, involving the hexaaquacobalt(II) ion, to illustrate
the process of ligand exchange. (2 marks)

Total: 9 marks

Answer to Question 1

(a) $[Ar]3d^6$ ✓

🖉 Remember that the 4s electrons are lost first. Three electrons are lost because the
cobalt ion is 3+.

(b) (i) Zinc (or iron) metal ✓. It will reduce Co^{3+} to Co^{2+}, because when its half-
equation is reversed and added to $Co^{3+} + e^- \longrightarrow Co^{2+}$, the $E^{\ominus}_{cell} = +0.76 + 1.82$ V,
which is positive, so the reaction will take place ✓. It will reduce Co^{2+} to Co,
as $E^{\ominus}_{cell} = +0.76 + (−0.28) = +0.48$ V is also positive ✓.

🖉 Reducing agents become oxidised and so appear on the *right* of reduction potential
half-equations. The reducing agents are therefore zinc, iron, tin and hydrogen peroxide.
However, the $E^{\ominus}$ value, as given in the data, must be smaller or more negative than
both −0.28 and +1.82. This narrows the choice to zinc or iron. To score full marks,
you must show that zinc (or iron) will *first* reduce cobalt(III) to cobalt(II) and *then*
cobalt(II) to cobalt(0). As the zinc half-equation is reversed, its sign must be changed
from −0.76 to +0.76 V.

(ii) The rate of the reaction may be too slow ✓. The conditions may be non-standard, such as concentrations not equal to 1 mol dm^{-3}, thereby altering the E values ✓.

(c) (i) $[Co(H_2O)_6]^{2+}$ ✓

(ii) $[Co(H_2O)_6]^{3+} + 6NH_3 \longrightarrow [Co(NH_3)_6]^{3+} + 6H_2O$ ✓✓

📝 This is the simplest example. A typical C-grade candidate would forget that the transition metal cations are hydrated with six water molecules. Another answer would be:

$[Co(H_2O)_6]^{2+} + 4Cl^- \longrightarrow [CoCl_4]^{2-} + 6H_2O$

Remember that as Cl^- is a large ligand, only four will fit round the cobalt ion.

■ ■ ■

Question 2

(a) State what is meant by the term *transition element*. (1 mark)

(b) Two reactions of chromium(III) chloride are outlined below.

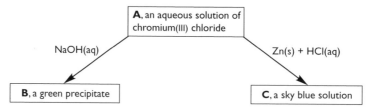

(i) Give *two* features of chromium chemistry, illustrated in the above scheme, that are typical of a transition element. (2 marks)

(ii) The formation of **B** from chromium(III) chloride is an example of deprotonation. Write an ionic equation for this process and use it to *explain* the term *deprotonation*. (3 marks)

(iii) Identify the chromium-containing species in solution **C**. (1 mark)

(c) Evaporating cold aqueous chromium(III) chloride produces violet crystals. However, when hot aqueous chromium(III) chloride crystallises, green crystals result. Both types of crystal have the same composition by mass: 19.5% chromium, 40.0% chlorine and 40.5% water.

(i) Show that the empirical formula of these two salts is $Cr(H_2O)_6Cl_3$. (2 marks)

(ii) The addition of excess aqueous silver nitrate to aqueous solutions of either of these two salts produces a precipitate of silver chloride, AgCl.

$Ag^+(aq) + Cl^-(aq) \longrightarrow AgCl(s)$

Under these conditions, all the chloride ions from the violet salt are precipitated, but only two-thirds from the green salt. Suggest formulae for the two salts, given that the water molecules may be either ligands in the complex ion or water of crystallisation, and that chloride ions could be ligands in the complex ion or separate, simple ions. (2 marks)

Total: **11 marks**

Answer to Question 2

(a) An element where at least one of its *ions* has a partially filled *d*-shell ✓.

(b) (i) Chromium has coloured ions (green and blue) ✓ and it has compounds in more than one oxidation state ✓.

🖉 A C-grade answer might quote transition element properties such as catalytic activity, which are not illustrated in the reaction scheme in the question.

(ii) $[Cr(H_2O)_6]^{3+} + 3OH^- \longrightarrow [Cr(H_2O)_3(OH)_3] + 3H_2O$ ✓✓
Each OH^- ion removes an H^+ ion from a ligand water molecule, so the reaction is deprotonation ✓.

(iii) The $[Cr(H_2O)_6]^{2+}$ ion ✓

🖉 You must always include the water ligands in deprotonation and ligand exchange reactions. C-grade answers often omit this. In (iii) you would have scored the mark for the name hexaaquachromium(II) ion.

(c) (i)

	Divide by r.a.m. ✓	Divide by smallest
Chromium	19.5/52 = 0.375	0.375/0.375 = 1
Chlorine	40/35.5 = 1.13	1.127/0.375 = 3
Water	40.5/18 = 2.25	2.25/0.375 = 6

The ratio is 1:3:6; therefore the empirical formula is $CrCl_3(H_2O)_6$ ✓.

(ii) The violet salt has all three chlorine ions outside the ligand sphere, so its formula is $[Cr(H_2O)_6]^{3+}3Cl^-$ ✓. The green salt has only $\frac{2}{3}$ of its chlorine outside the ligand sphere, so is $[Cr(H_2O)_5Cl]^{2+}2Cl^-.H_2O$ ✓.

■ ■ ■

Question 3

(a) (i) Explain what is meant by the following terms:
  - rate of reaction
  - overall order of reaction   (2 marks)

(ii) Explain why the order of reaction cannot be deduced from the stoichiometric equation for a reaction.   (1 mark)

(b) Substitution reactions of halogenoalkanes can proceed via an S_N1 or S_N2 mechanism. When 1-bromobutane, $CH_3CH_2CH_2CH_2Br$, 2-bromobutane, $CH_3CH_2CHBrCH_3$, and 2-bromo-2-methylpropane, $(CH_3)_3CBr$, are reacted separately with aqueous sodium hydroxide, each gives the corresponding alcohol.

(i) Give the mechanism for the S_N1 reaction between 2-bromobutane and hydroxide ions.   (3 marks)

(ii) Explain why the product mixture is not optically active.   (2 marks)

(iii) In an experiment designed to find the mechanism of the reaction between 2-bromo-2-methylpropane and hydroxide ions, the following data were obtained at constant temperature:

Initial concentration of 2-bromo-2-methylpropane/ mol dm^{-3}	Initial concentration of OH$^-$/mol dm^{-3}	Initial rate of reaction/ mol dm^{-3} s^{-1}
0.10	0.10	1.2×10^{-2}
0.20	0.10	2.4×10^{-2}
0.30	0.20	3.6×10^{-2}

Use the data to deduce the rate equation for the reaction of 2-bromo-2-methylpropane and sodium hydroxide. (3 marks)

(c) Suggest, in outline, a method you could use to follow the progress of the reaction between a bromoalkane and aqueous sodium hydroxide. (3 marks)

Total: 14 marks

Answer to Question 3

(a) (i) The rate of reaction is the rate of change of the concentration of a reactant or product ✓ (or the amount the concentration of a reactant changes with time). The overall order of reaction is the sum of the powers to which the concentration terms are raised in the rate equation ✓.

🖉 The rate is *not* the time taken for the reaction to go to completion. It could be useful to give an example to add to the explanation of order, such as if the rate equation is rate = $k[A]^1[B]^2$, the order is 3.

(ii) The order of reaction depends on the mechanism, as only those substances that react before or in the *rate-determining step* appear in the rate equation ✓.

🖉 A typical C-grade answer would state that orders must be determined experimentally, without explaining why.

(b) (i)

🖉 Marks are awarded for:
- 1st arrow ✓
- intermediate with charge ✓
- arrow from O of OH$^-$ ✓

Arrows must start from bonds or atoms and never from minus signs.

(ii) The intermediate is planar and is attacked in the second step from either side ✓. Therefore, a racemic (50/50) mixture of the two optical isomers is produced ✓.

(iii) Comparing experiment 1 and 2, the concentration of the bromo- compound is doubled and that of hydroxide ions is kept constant. The rate also doubles. Therefore, the reaction is first-order with respect to the bromo- compound ✓.
    Comparing experiments 1 and 3, the concentration of the bromo- compound trebles, which would cause the rate to treble. The rate trebles and therefore the doubling of the hydroxide ion concentration has no effect. This means that the reaction is zero-order with respect to OH⁻ ions ✓. Rate = k[bromo- compound] ✓

📝 Remember to include the rate constant, k, in your overall rate equation. C-grade answers might fail to show enough working. For example, 'if you double the concentration of the bromo- compound, the rate will double, but doubling the concentration of hydroxide ions will have no effect. Thus, rate = k[bromo]'.

(c) Mix the two solutions and start the clock, removing samples at known times ✓. Drop the samples into iced water to stop the reaction ✓. Titrate the sodium hydroxide against a solution of acid ✓.

📝 There are several ways to follow this reaction. The simplest is described above. Answers in terms of following pH would score 1 mark only, since the change in pH is insignificant until right at the end of the reaction.

■ ■ ■

Question 4

(a) Benzene, C_6H_6, reacts with ethanoyl chloride, CH_3COCl, to give a compound of molecular formula C_8H_8O.
   (i)   Identify another substance that must be present for this reaction to occur and state the function of this substance in the reaction.   (2 marks)
   (ii) Give the mechanism for this reaction.   (4 marks)
(b) Phenol, C_6H_5OH, reacts differently from benzene with ethanoyl chloride. State the type of reaction that would occur between phenol and ethanoyl chloride and give the structure of the organic product.   (2 marks)
(c) A benzene ring containing two hydroxy groups, $C_6H_4(OH)_2$, can exist as a range of isomers.
   (i)   Draw the structure of each isomer.   (2 marks)
   (ii) A polymer can be formed by reacting one of these isomers with the diacyl chloride $ClCOCH_2COCl$. Draw a diagram indicating clearly the structure of such a polymer.   (2 marks)
(d) The compound 4-hydroxyazobenzene has the formula:

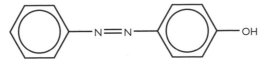

It can be obtained from phenylamine and phenol in two steps. Identify the intermediate formed and give the reagents and conditions for each step.   (4 marks)

Total: 16 marks

Answer to Question 4

(a) (i) The other substance needed is anhydrous aluminium chloride (or iron(III) chloride) ✓. It functions as a catalyst ✓.

(ii) $CH_3COCl + AlCl_3 \longrightarrow CH_3CO^+ + AlCl_4^-$ ✓

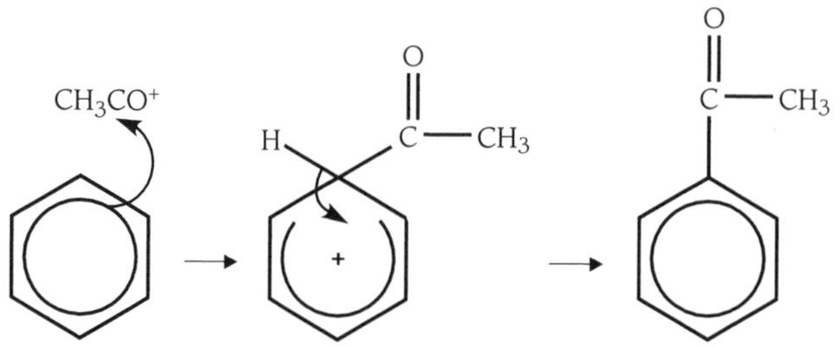

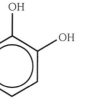

💡 Marks are awarded for:

- 1st arrow ✓
- intermediate ✓
- 2nd arrow ✓

The first arrow must go towards the carbon atom in the carbonyl group. The broken ring in the intermediate must cover five carbon atoms.

(b) Esterification ✓

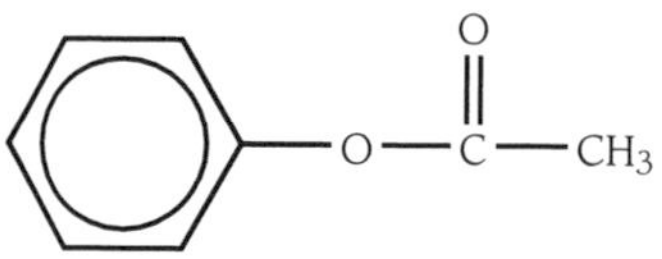

💡 Three correct formulae score 2 marks and two score 1 mark. Just one correct formula is not enough for a mark.

(c) (i)

(ii)

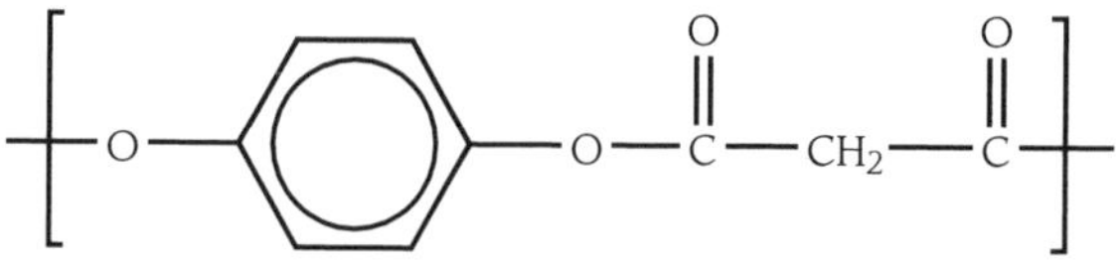

📝 Marks are awarded for:
  • ester link ✓
  • correct formula of polymer ✓

(d) The intermediate is benzene diazonium ion (formula $C_6H_5N^+\equiv N$) ✓. The reagents for the first step are sodium nitrite and dilute hydrochloric acid ✓. The conditions are: a temperature between 0°C and 10°C ✓; and, for the second step, that phenol must be in sodium hydroxide solution ✓.

📝 Do not give nitrous acid as the reagent in step 1 because it is not a chemical that can be taken off the shelf — it decomposes at room temperature.

■ ■ ■

Question 5

(a) Use the concepts of the different types of covalent bond and of bond enthalpy to explain the structure of the benzene ring. (5 marks)

(b) Outline how a sample of pure benzene, C_6H_6 (boiling temperature 80°C), could be converted to a pure sample of nitrobenzene, $C_6H_5NO_2$ (boiling temperature 211°C). Include in your answer the reagents and conditions involved and the technique for obtaining a sample of pure nitrobenzene from the reaction mixture. (5 marks)

Total: 10 marks

Answer to Question 5

(a) The formula of C_6H_6 might suggest that the molecule has alternate double and single bonds ✓. If so, its enthalpy of formation, based on the sum of the bond enthalpies of three single and three double bonds and six C–H bond enthalpies ✓, gives a value that is more than the actual measured value ✓. Its structure is a ring of six carbon atoms, with each carbon bonded with σ-bonds to each of its neighbours ✓, and a delocalised π-cloud of electrons above and below the plane of the ring ✓.

📝 The answer must be in terms of *types* of covalent bond (σ and π) and bond enthalpies (C–C, C=C, C–H). Comparison must be made between benzene, with its delocalised system, and the theoretical molecule with alternate single and double bonds.

(b) The reagents are a mixture of concentrated nitric ✓ and concentrated sulphuric acids ✓. The conditions are in a warm water bath to a maximum 50°C ✓. To obtain pure nitrobenzene, add water and separate off the organic layer using a separating funnel ✓. Dry, and fractionally distil off the benzene, collecting the fraction boiling at 211°C ✓.

■ ■ ■

Question 6

The pain-relieving drug ibuprofen has the formula:

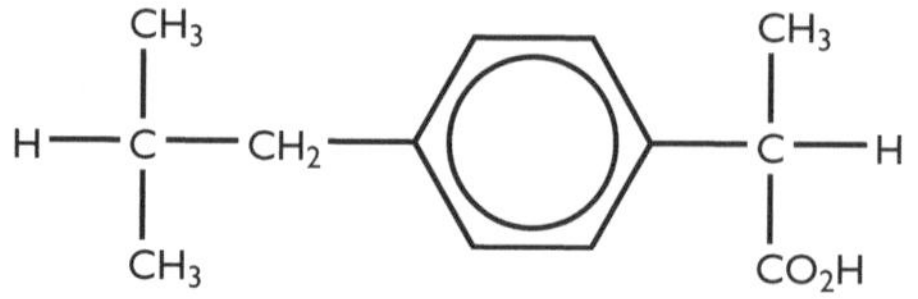

$$H-\overset{\overset{\displaystyle CH_3}{|}}{\underset{\underset{\displaystyle CH_3}{|}}{C}}-CH_2- \bigcirc -\overset{\overset{\displaystyle CH_3}{|}}{\underset{\underset{\displaystyle CO_2H}{|}}{C}}-H$$

(a) A molecule of this compound is chiral. Explain, with the aid of diagrams, how two optical isomers result from a chiral centre. Identify the chiral centre and explain how these isomers could be distinguished from each other.
(4 marks)

(b) Compounds A and B, shown below, are used as intermediates in the manufacture of ibuprofen.

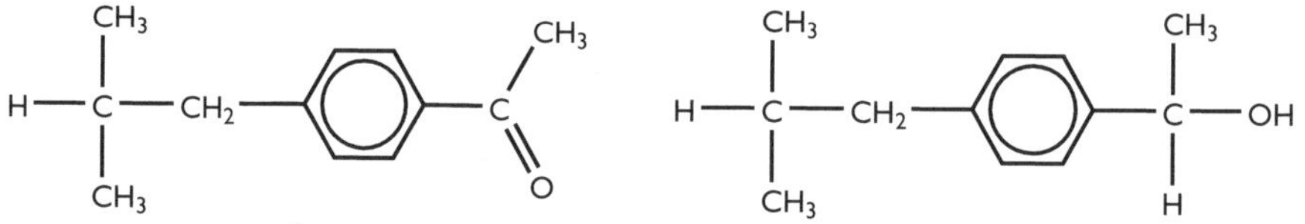

$$H-\overset{\overset{\displaystyle CH_3}{|}}{\underset{\underset{\displaystyle CH_3}{|}}{C}}-CH_2- \bigcirc -\overset{\displaystyle C}{\underset{\displaystyle \parallel O}{}}{}^{CH_3}$$

A

$$H-\overset{\overset{\displaystyle CH_3}{|}}{\underset{\underset{\displaystyle CH_3}{|}}{C}}-CH_2- \bigcirc -\overset{\overset{\displaystyle CH_3}{|}}{\underset{\underset{\displaystyle H}{|}}{C}}-OH$$

B

(i) Suggest a simple chemical test that would distinguish between A and B.
(2 marks)

(ii) If *either* A *or* B is heated with a mixture of aqueous sodium hydroxide and potassium manganate(VII) solution, the same compound is produced. Suggest the structure of this compound.
(2 marks)

(c) A tablet of ibuprofen contains a very small quantity of the drug while the remainder of the tablet material is unreactive. In an analysis, 50 tablets were reacted with 100.0 cm³ of 1.00 mol dm⁻³ aqueous sodium hydroxide, an excess. The ibuprofen reacted as a weak acid. When the reaction was complete, the remaining aqueous sodium hydroxide was titrated with 2.00 mol dm⁻³ hydrochloric acid. 25.75 cm³ of the acid were required for neutralisation.

(i) Calculate the mass, in mg, of ibuprofen in *one* tablet. (M_r ibuprofen = 206)
(5 marks)

(ii) Calculate the number of molecules of ibuprofen that this tablet represents. (Avogadro constant = 6.023×10^{23} mol⁻¹)
(2 marks)

Total: 15 marks

Answer to Question 6

(a)

where R is H

They can be distinguished because they will *rotate* the plane of plane-polarised light in opposite directions ✓.

🖉 There is 1 mark for circling the chiral carbon and 1 mark for each isomer. There is no need to use ibuprofen as your example — something simple, such as 2-hydroxypropanoic acid, would do. Whatever you use, you must mark the chiral centre (put a ring around it) and draw both isomers in three dimensions so that they are mirror images of each other. Make sure that the bonds go to the correct atoms, such as the oxygen of an –OH group and the carbon of a –CH$_3$ or –COOH group. Do *not* say that optical isomers *reflect, refract or bend* plane-polarised light.

(b) (i) • Show that A is a carbonyl compound by adding 2,4-dinitrophenyl-hydrazine ✓. Compound A will give an orange precipitate and B will not ✓.
  or
  • Show that B has an –OH group by adding phosphorus pentachloride ✓. Compound B will give steamy fumes and A will not react ✓.

🖉 Two alternative answers are given. C-grade answers would fail to say what *both* substances would do in the test and so lose the second mark.

(ii) The product is HOOCC$_6$H$_4$COOH ✓✓ or its disodium salt, NaOOCC$_6$H$_4$COONa.

🖉 Oxidising only one side chain to a COOH (or COONa) group would score 1 mark.

(c) (i) Amount of HCl = amount of NaOH left = 2.00 × 25.75/1000 = 0.0515 mol ✓
Original amount of NaOH = 1.00 × 100/1000 = 0.100 mol
Amount NaOH reacted with tablets = 0.100 – 0.0515 = 0.0485 mol ✓
Amount of ibuprofen in 50 tablets = 0.0485 mol
Amount of ibuprofen in 1 tablet = 0.0485/50 = 9.70 × 10^{-4} mol ✓
Mass of ibuprofen in 1 tablet = 9.7 × 10^{-4} × 206 = 0.1998 g ✓
$$= 0.1998 \times 1000 = 199.8 \text{ mg}$$
$$= 200 \text{ mg (to 3 significant figures)} ✓$$

🖉 The route is: amount of HCl in titration ⟶ amount of left-over NaOH ⟶ amount of NaOH reacted with acid group in ibuprofen ⟶ amount of ibuprofen. All reactions are in a 1:1 ratio. Don't forget to convert your mass in grams to a mass in milligrams, as required by the question.

(ii) Number of molecules = moles × Avogadro's constant
$$= 9.70 \times 10^{-4} \text{ mol} \times 6.023 \times 10^{23} \text{ mol}^{-1} ✓ = 5.84 \times 10^{20} ✓$$

🖉 The number of molecules is *always* a huge number, unlike the number of moles.

Unit Test 5, June 2002

Question 1

The equation for the reaction between persulphate ions and iodide ions is:

$$S_2O_8^{2-} + 2I^- \longrightarrow 2SO_4^{2-} + I_2$$

In an experiment to determine the rate of reaction between persulphate ions and iodide ions in aqueous solution, the following data were obtained:

$[S_2O_8^{2-}]$/mol dm^{-3}	$[I^-]$/mol dm^{-3}	Initial rate/mol dm^{-3} s^{-1}
0.100	0.100	0.36
0.200	0.100	0.72
0.200	0.200	1.44

(a) (i) Deduce the order of reaction with respect to each of the reagents and hence write the rate equation for the reaction. (3 marks)

  (ii) With reference to this reaction, state what is meant by the *overall order* of a reaction. (1 mark)

  (iii) Calculate the rate constant, including units. (2 marks)

(b) (i) Suggest a suitable experimental technique that would enable you to determine the rate of the reaction. (1 mark)

  (ii) Suggest a necessary condition that would help to ensure accurate results. (1 mark)

Total: 8 marks

Answer to Question 1

(a) (i) In experiments 1 and 2, the concentration of $S_2O_8^{2-}$ doubles, while that of I^- stays constant. The rate also doubles. Therefore, the reaction is first-order with respect to $S_2O_8^{2-}$ ions ✓.

  In experiments 2 and 3, the concentration of I^- doubles, while that of $S_2O_8^{2-}$ stays constant. The rate also doubles. Therefore, the reaction is also first-order with respect to I^- ions ✓.

  The rate equation is: rate = $k[S_2O_8^{2-}][I^-]$ ✓

☞ A C-grade answer might fail to give any working to show the partial orders. The question says 'deduce', so some explanation must be given.

  (ii) The overall order is the sum of the powers of the concentration terms in the rate equation, which is $1 + 1 = 2$ ✓.

  (iii) The rate constant $k = \dfrac{\text{rate}}{[S_2O_8^{2-}][I^-]}$

  $= \dfrac{0.36 \text{ mol dm}^{-3} \text{ s}^{-1}}{0.100 \text{ mol dm}^{-3} \times 0.100 \text{ mol dm}^{-3}} = 36 \text{ mol}^{-1} \text{ dm}^3 \text{ s}^{-1}$ ✓✓

(b) (i) • Remove samples at regular intervals and titrate with sodium thiosulphate solution ✓.

or

• Using a colorimeter, measure the degree of colour of the iodine in the solution at regular intervals ✓.

Two alternative answers are given. There is only 1 mark for this, so don't give masses of detail. The key concepts are the method (titration or colorimeter) and the substance used for monitoring (sodium thiosulphate or degree of colour of iodine).

(ii) The reaction must be carried out at constant temperature ✓.

■ ■ ■

Question 2

Alkenes undergo electrophilic addition whereas arenes, such as benzene, undergo electrophilic substitution.

(a) What is an electrophile? (1 mark)

(b) Propene, CH_3–$CH=CH_2$, reacts with HBr to give $CH_3CHBrCH_3$ as the major product.

    (i) **What is the name of the compound $CH_3CHBrCH_3$?** (1 mark)

    (ii) **Give the mechanism for the reaction.** (3 marks)

    (iii) **Explain why the major product is $CH_3CHBrCH_3$ rather than**

           $CH_3CH_2CH_2Br$. (2 marks)

(c) Benzene, C_6H_6, reacts with CH_3Br to give $C_6H_5CH_3$.

    (i) **What catalyst might be used in this reaction?** (1 mark)

    (ii) **Give the mechanism for the reaction. You should include the step**

           that forms the electrophile. (4 marks)

(d) Explain, in terms of structure and bonding, why benzene and propene react differently with electrophiles. (4 marks)

Total: 16 marks

Answer to Question 2

(a) A species that attacks an electron-rich site and accepts a pair of electrons from that site, forming a covalent bond ✓.

It is essential that you define an electrophile (or a nucleophile) in terms of electrons and bond formation.

(b) (i) 2-bromopropane ✓

    (ii)

📝 Marks are awarded for:
- both arrows in step 1 ✓
- intermediate ✓
- arrow from Br⁻ in step 2 ✓

In the first step, the curly arrow must go from the π-bond towards the H of HBr. This shows that the H atom (which is δ⁺) in HBr is the electrophile. It accepts the π-electrons from the double bond and forms a σ-bond with the primary carbon atom. The other curly arrow must go from the σ-bond in HBr to the Br. The arrow in the second step must *not* go from the minus sign of the Br⁻ ion.

(iii) The major product is 2-bromopropane because the intermediate formed, $CH_3CH^+CH_3$, is a secondary carbocation ✓ which is more stable than the primary carbocation, $CH_3CH_2CH_2^+$, which would be formed if $CH_3CH_2CH_2Br$ were the product ✓.

(c) (i) The catalyst is anhydrous aluminium chloride ✓.

(ii) $CH_3Br + AlCl_3 \longrightarrow CH_3^+ + AlBrCl_3$ ✓

📝 Marks are awarded for:
- 1st arrow ✓
- intermediate ✓
- 2nd arrow ✓

In the first step, the arrow must start on the delocalised ring and go towards the C of the CH_3^+ ion. In the intermediate, the partial ring must go across five carbon atoms and the arrow must start from the σ C–H bond and go inside the benzene ring.

(d) A catalyst is needed for the electrophilic reactions of benzene as the π-bond in benzene is stronger than the π-bond in propene ✓, because of the delocalised ✓ π-system in benzene.

In benzene, the second step is the elimination of H⁺ rather than the addition of Br⁻ because this enables the delocalisation energy to be preserved ✓, whereas in propene, addition is energetically more favourable ✓.

📝 The first 2 marks are for explaining the difference in the rates of attack by the electrophile, and the last 2 marks for the difference in stability of the π-systems of the two organic molecules. A common failing in C-grade answers would be to concentrate solely on benzene and not to compare it with propene.

■ ■ ■

Question 3

(a) Complete the electronic structure of a scandium atom, a chromium atom and a Cr³⁺ ion.

$$3d \qquad 4s$$

Sc [Ar] ☐☐☐☐☐ ☐

Cr [Ar] ☐☐☐☐☐ ☐

Cr³⁺ [Ar] ☐☐☐☐☐ ☐

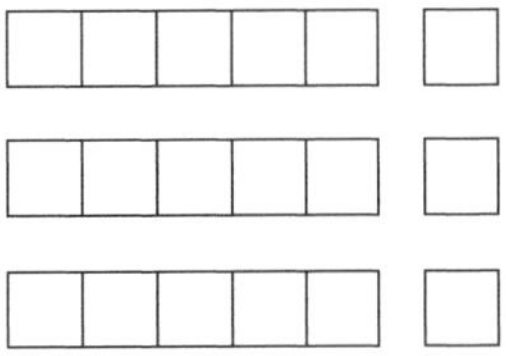

(3 marks)

(b) Both scandium and chromium are *d-block* elements, but only chromium is a *transition* element. Explain the meaning of these two terms. (2 marks)

(c) Cr^{3+} exists in aqueous solution as the green ion $[Cr(H_2O)_6]^{3+}$.

(i) Draw the $[Cr(H_2O)_6]^{3+}$ ion to show its shape clearly. (1 mark)

(ii) Explain the origin of the colour in $[Cr(H_2O)_6]^{3+}$. (3 marks)

(d) (i) State what you would see if aqueous sodium hydroxide were added drop by drop to a solution of $[Cr(H_2O)_6]^{3+}$ until the sodium hydroxide was in excess. (2 marks)

(ii) What type of reaction is occurring in (d) (i)? (1 mark)

Total: 12 marks

Answer to Question 3

(a)

$$3d \qquad\qquad 4s$$

Sc [Ar] [↑ ☐☐☐☐] [↑↓] ✓

Cr [Ar] [↑ ↑ ↑ ↑ ↑] [↑] ✓

Cr³⁺ [Ar] [↑ ↑ ↑ ☐☐] ☐ ✓

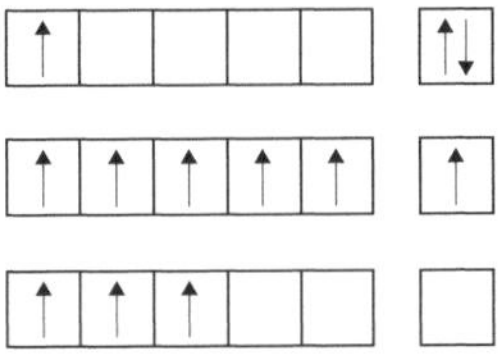

(b) A *d*-block element is one in which the last electron has gone into a *d*-orbital ✓. A transition element has one or more of its ions with an incomplete *d*-shell ✓.

(c) (i) The shape of the ion is octahedral.

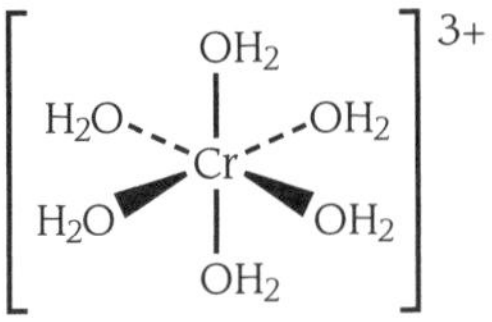

$$
\left[
\begin{array}{c}
OH_2 \\
H_2O\text{---}Cr\text{---}OH_2 \\
H_2O \qquad OH_2 \\
OH_2
\end{array}
\right]^{3+}
$$

📝 It is always a good idea to give the name of the shape that you have drawn, in case your diagram is not very good. Make sure that the ligands are bonded to the chromium ion through the oxygen in the water molecule.

(ii) The *d*-orbitals are split by the ligands into three of lower energy and two of higher energy ✓. When illuminated by white light, an electron absorbs some of the light energy ✓ and jumps from the *lower* to the higher level ✓.

(d) (i) The green solution would first form a green precipitate ✓, which forms a dark green solution with excess sodium hydroxide solution ✓.

 (ii) The reaction is an example of deprotonation ✓.

■ ■ ■

Question 4

The following standard electrode potentials will be required in answering this question:

	$E^{\ominus}$/V
$Zn^{2+} + 2e^- \rightleftharpoons Zn$	−0.76
$V^{3+} + e^- \rightleftharpoons V^{2+}$	−0.26
$SO_4^{2-} + 2e^- + 2H^+ \rightleftharpoons SO_3^{2-} + H_2O$	+0.17
$VO^{2+} + 2H^+ + e^- \rightleftharpoons V^{3+} + H_2O$	+0.34
$VO_2^+ + 2H^+ + e^- \rightleftharpoons VO^{2+} + H_2O$	+1.00

(a) Give the colours of the following ions: VO_2^+, VO^{2+}, V^{3+}, V^{2+}. (2 marks)

(b) (i) Derive the overall equation for the reduction of VO_2^+ to VO^{2+} by zinc in acid solution. (2 marks)

 (ii) Give the formula of the vanadium species that would result if VO_2^+ ions were reduced by sulphite ions, SO_3^{2-}. Explain your answer. (3 marks)

(c) Disproportionation requires an atom to have at least three oxidation states.

 (i) Explain why this is so. (1 mark)

 (ii) Derive an equation for the disproportionation of VO^{2+} into VO_2^+ and V^{3+}. (2 marks)

Total: 10 marks

Answer to Question 4

(a) VO_2^+ is yellow, VO^{2+} is blue, V^{3+} is green and V^{2+} is lavender (mauve) ✓✓.

All four colours correct scores 2 marks; any two correct score 1 mark.

(b) (i) Reverse the Zn^{2+}/Zn equation and add it to *2 times* the VO_2^+/VO^{2+} equation:
$$2VO_2^+ + Zn + 4H^+ \longrightarrow 2VO^{2+} + 2H_2O + Zn^{2+} \checkmark\checkmark$$

There is 1 mark for all the species in the equation and 1 mark for balancing the equation. The reactants are Zn and VO_2^+ and so must be on the *left* of the overall equation. The VO_2^+/VO^{2+} equation has to be doubled so that the electrons cancel with those in the zinc half-equation.

(ii) The vanadium product would be V^{3+} ✓ because the electrode potential for VO_2^+/VO^{2+} with SO_3^{2-}/SO_4^{2-} is $+1.00 - (+0.17) = +0.83$ V and for VO^{2+}/V^{3+} with SO_3^{2-}/SO_4^{2-} is $+0.34 - (+0.17) = +0.17$ V. Both are positive, so both reactions occur ✓. However, $E^\ominus$ for V^{3+}/V^{2+} with SO_3^{2-}/SO_4^{2-} would be $-0.26 - (+0.17) = -0.43$ V, which is negative. Therefore, SO_3^{2-} will not reduce V^{3+} to V^{2+} ✓.

📝 You have to work out the sign of $E^\ominus_{cell}$ for SO_3^{2-} ions reducing VO_2^+ to VO^{2+}, VO^{2+} to V^{3+} and V^{3+} to V^{2+}. Remember that $E^\ominus_{cell} = E^\ominus$ (oxidising agent) $- E^\ominus$ (reducing agent).

(c) (i) Disproportionation requires the original oxidation state of an element both to rise and fall ✓.

(ii) Adding the VO^{2+}/V^{3+} half-equation to the reversed VO_2^+/VO^{2+} half equation:
$$2VO^{2+} \longrightarrow VO_2^+ + V^{3+}$$

📝 There is 1 mark for the species and 1 mark for balancing the equation. The only reactant is VO^{2+}, so you need to find two equations with it on the left.

■ ■ ■

Question 5

(a) Pure copper is needed for electrical applications. The purity of a sample of copper can be found by reacting it with concentrated nitric acid, neutralising the resultant solution and then treating it with excess potassium iodide. Iodine is liberated and this can be titrated with standard sodium thiosulphate solution. The reactions are:
$$Cu(s) + 4HNO_3(l) \longrightarrow Cu(NO_3)_2(aq) + 2NO_2(g) + 2H_2O(l)$$
$$2Cu^{2+}(aq) + 4I^-(aq) \longrightarrow 2CuI(s) + I_2(aq)$$
A copper foil electrode from an electric cell weighed 1.74 g. It was converted into 250 cm^3 of a solution of copper ions. Excess iodide ions were added to 25.0 cm^3 of this solution and the mixture was titrated with 0.100 mol dm^{-3} sodium thiosulphate solution. On average, 26.8 cm^3 were required. Calculate the purity of the copper foil. *(6 marks)*

(b) Phenylamine can be converted into benzenediazonium chloride which can then be decomposed in acid solution using a copper(I) chloride catalyst.
$$C_6H_5N_2^+Cl^- \longrightarrow C_6H_5Cl + N_2$$

(i) The catalytic effect of transition metals or their ions is often attributed to their having several stable oxidation states. Explain why such states are possible in transition metals and why they are important in catalysis. *(4 marks)*

(ii) Phenylamine is prepared from benzene. Give the reagents and conditions needed for each of the steps in the conversion. *(6 marks)*

Total: 16 marks

Answer to Question 5

(a) The equation for the reaction between sodium thiosulphate and iodine is:
$$2S_2O_3^{2-} + I_2 \longrightarrow S_4O_6^{2-} + 2I^- \checkmark$$
Amount of sodium thiosulphate $= 0.100 \times 26.8/1000 = 2.68 \times 10^{-3}$ mol $\checkmark$
Amount of iodine, $I_2 = \frac{1}{2} \times 2.68 \times 10^{-3}$ mol
Amount of copper $= 2 \times$ amount of $I_2 = 2 \times \frac{1}{2} \times 2.68 \times 10^{-3}$ mol $= 2.68 \times 10^{-3}$ mol $\checkmark$
Total amount of copper $= 10 \times 2.68 \times 10^{-3} = 2.68 \times 10^{-2}$ mol $\checkmark$
Mass of copper $= 2.68 \times 10^{-2}$ mol $\times 63.5$ g mol$^{-1} = 1.70$ g $\checkmark$
Purity of copper $= 1.70 \times 100/1.74 = 97.8\%$ $\checkmark$

You must give the equation for the reaction between thiosulphate and iodine, so that you can convert the titration data to the amount of iodine produced. The ratio of Cu^{2+} reacted (and hence Cu) to I_2 produced is 2:1, so the amount of copper is twice the amount of iodine. Make sure that you give your answer to *three* significant figures to match the data given.

(b) (i) The increase in successive ionisation energies of the transition elements is similar $\checkmark$ and is compensated for by the extra hydration energy of the more charged cation (or compensated for by the bond energy in the anion) $\checkmark$. Catalysis involves the metal ion moving from one oxidation state to another $\checkmark$ and then back again $\checkmark$ as the catalyst is regenerated.

(ii) The first step is to convert benzene to nitrobenzene $\checkmark$. This is carried out at 50°C $\checkmark$ using concentrated nitric and sulphuric acids $\checkmark$. Nitrobenzene is reduced to phenylamine by heating $\checkmark$ it with tin $\checkmark$ and concentrated hydrochloric acid $\checkmark$.

■ ■ ■

Question 6

Consider the following reaction scheme:

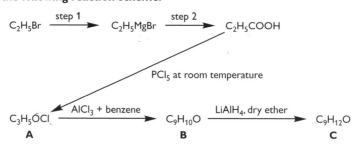

(a) Give the reagents and conditions for:
  (i) Step 1 – Potassium manganate (VII)   (2 marks)
  (ii) Step 2 – Potassium dichromate (VI)   (2 marks)
(b) Give the equation for the reaction between propanoic acid and phosphorus pentachloride, making clear the structure of compound A.   (2 marks)

(c) Compound **B** reacts with 2,4-dinitrophenylhydrazine but not with ammoniacal silver nitrate solution. Give the structural formula for compound **B** and explain why **B** reacts with 2,4-dinitrophenylhydrazine but not with ammoniacal silver nitrate. (3 marks)

(d) (i) Give the structural formula for **C**. (1 mark)

    (ii) State why the ether solvent must be dry in the conversion of **B** to **C**. (1 mark)

(e) The infrared spectra of **B** and **C** are given below, together with a table of infrared absorption.

Compound B:

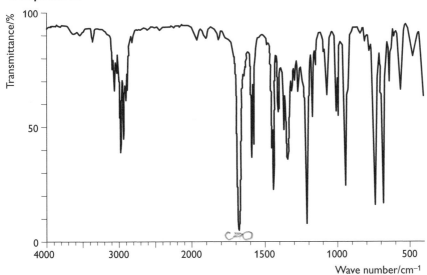

Compound C:

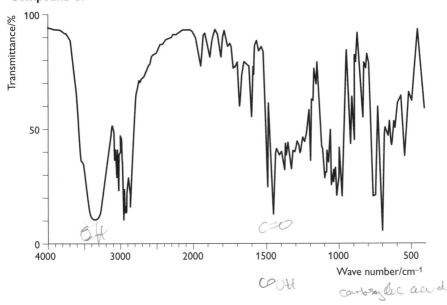

Infrared absorptions:

Bond	Assignment	Wave number/cm⁻¹
C–H	Alkanes	2850–2950
	Alkenes, arenes	3000–3100
C=C	Alkenes	1610–1680
Benzene ring	Arenes	1450–1650
C=O	Aldehydes, ketones, amides, esters, carboxylic acids	1680–1750
O–H	Free	3580–3670
	Hydrogen bonded in alcohols	3230–3550
	Hydrogen bonded in acids	2500–3300

What is the evidence from these spectra for the conversion of the functional group in B to that in C? (2 marks)

Total: 13 marks

Answer to Question 6

(a) (i) The reagent is magnesium ✓ and the conditions are dry ether ✓.
(ii) The reagents are dry, solid carbon dioxide ✓ followed by dilute hydrochloric acid ✓.

In all reactions of Grignard reagents, the intermediate has to be hydrolysed by dilute acid to give the final organic product, which here is a carboxylic acid.

(b)

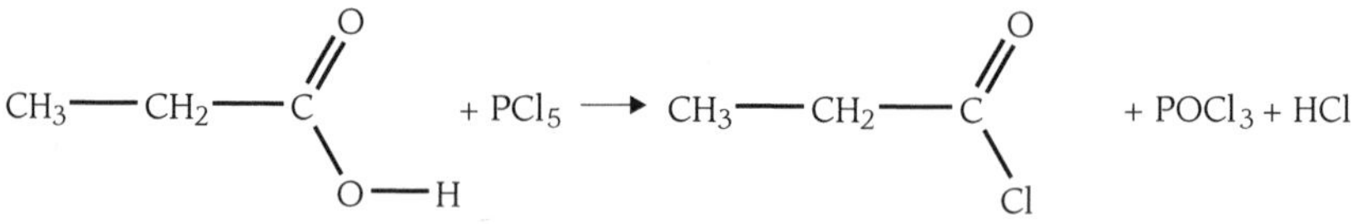

$$CH_3\text{---}CH_2\text{---}C(\text{=O})(O\text{---}H) + PCl_5 \longrightarrow CH_3\text{---}CH_2\text{---}C(\text{=O})(Cl) + POCl_3 + HCl$$

There is 1 mark for the correct products and 1 mark for showing the structure of the acid chloride, with the COCl group written out to show the bonds.

(c)

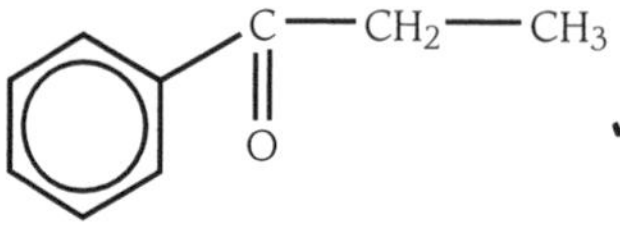

$C_6H_5\text{---}C(\text{=O})\text{---}CH_2\text{---}CH_3$ ✓

2,4-dinitrophenylhydrazine reacts with the carbonyl group present in B ✓. B is a ketone and so does not react with ammoniacal silver nitrate because it cannot be oxidised ✓.

You should realise that the reaction of A to B is the Friedel–Crafts reaction between benzene and an acid chloride to give a ketone.

(d) (i)

OH
|
C—CH$_2$—CH$_3$ ✓
|
H
(with a benzene ring attached to the C)

🖉 Lithium aluminium hydride reduces C=O groups in carbonyl compounds, acids and esters, but it does *not* reduce C=C in alkenes or in benzene rings.

(ii) The lithium aluminium hydride would react with the water ✓.

(e) The ketone B has an absorption peak at 1700 cm^{-1} owing to the carbonyl group. However, it does not have a peak around 3300 cm^{-1} because it does not have an –OH group ✓. The alcohol C has no peak around 1700 cm^{-1} because the carbonyl group has been reduced to an –OH group, which shows as a broad peak at 3300 cm^{-1} ✓.

🖉 You must make some comparison between the two spectra, relating the chemical change (C=O group to CH(OH) group) to the spectra.

The periodic table

Group

Period	1	2												3	4	5	6	7	0
1	1 H 1																		4 He 2
2	7 Li 3	9 Be 4												11 B 5	12 C 6	14 N 7	16 O 8	19 F 9	20 Ne 10
3	23 Na 11	24 Mg 12												27 Al 13	28 Si 14	31 P 15	32 S 16	35.5 Cl 17	40 Ar 18
4	39 K 19	40 Ca 20	45 Sc 21	48 Ti 22	51 V 23	52 Cr 24	55 Mn 25	56 Fe 26	59 Co 27	59 Ni 28	63.5 Cu 29	65.4 Zn 30		70 Ga 31	73 Ge 32	75 As 33	79 Se 34	80 Br 35	84 Kr 36
5	85 Rb 37	88 Sr 38	89 Y 39	91 Zr 40	93 Nb 41	96 Mo 42	99 Tc 43	101 Ru 44	103 Rh 45	106 Pd 46	108 Ag 47	112 Cd 48		115 In 49	119 Sn 50	122 Sb 51	128 Te 52	127 I 53	131 Xe 54
6	133 Cs 55	137 Ba 56	139 La 57	178 Hf 72	181 Ta 73	184 W 74	186 Re 75	190 Os 76	192 Ir 77	195 Pt 78	197 Au 79	201 Hg 80		204 Tl 81	207 Pb 82	209 Bi 83	210 Po 84	210 At 85	222 Rn 86
7	223 Fr 87	226 Ra 88	227 Ac 89																

Key:

Molar mass/g mol^{-1}
Symbol
Atomic number

140 Ce 58	141 Pr 59	144 Nd 60	(147) Pm 61	150 Sm 62	152 Eu 63	157 Gd 64	159 Tb 65	163 Dy 66	165 Ho 67	167 Er 68	169 Tm 69	173 Yb 70	175 Lu 71
232 Th 90	(231) Pa 91	238 U 92	(237) Np 93	(242) Pu 94	(243) Am 95	(247) Cm 96	(245) Bk 97	(251) Cf 98	(254) Es 99	(253) Fm 100	(256) Md 101	(254) No 102	(257) Lr 103